# Straight Talk,
*No Chaser*

**ALSO BY STEVE HARVEY**

*Act Like a Lady, Think Like a Man*

# HOW TO FIND,

## KEEP,

## AND UNDERSTAND

## A MAN

# Straight Talk, *No Chaser*

➤━◆━◄

# STEVE HARVEY

WITH *Denene Millner*

Amistad

*An Imprint of HarperCollinsPublishers*

HarperCollins books may be purchased for educational, business, or sales promotional use. For information, please e-mail the Special Markets Department at SPsales@harpercollins.com.

A hardcover edition of this book was published in 2011 by Amistad, an imprint of HarperCollins Publishers.

FIRST AMISTAD PAPERBACK EDITION PUBLISHED 2012.

The Library of Congress has catalogued the hardcover edition as follows:
Harvey, Steve.
    Straight talk, no chaser: how to find, keep, and understand a man / by Steve Harvey with Denene Millner. — 1st ed.
        p.   cm.
    Summary: "More relationship advice in this much-anticipated follow-up to the number one *New York Times* bestseller and international sensation *Act Like a Lady, Think Like a Man*" — Provided by publisher.
    ISBN 978-0-06-172899-0 (Hardcover)
    ISBN 978-0-06-200369-0 (International Edition)
    1. Man-woman relationships. 2. Men—Psychology. 3. Mate selection.
I. Millner, Denene. II. Title.
HQ801.H352497   2011
306.7—dc22                                              2010044105

ISBN 978-0-06-172896-9 (pbk.)

        14   15   16      OV/RRD      10   9   8   7

This book is dedicated to the memory of my beloved mother,
ELOISE VERA HARVEY,
who taught me my love and faith in GOD,
and to my father,
JESSE "SLICK" HARVEY,
whose sole purpose seemed to be to teach me how to be a man.
That combination has kept me moving forward
even in my darkest days. . . .
I miss them so much. I hope I'm making them proud.

# CONTENTS

# INTRODUCTION

>———◆———‹———

I can hear her heels clicking on the cement, coming faster and faster, louder and louder. She was working her way up three levels of the circular parking lot—she's skipped the elevators altogether and is running in the middle of the road trying to run me down before I make it to my car or to stop me if I start to drive away. Just as I am about to duck into the backseat, she catches me: "Steve Harvey! Steve Harvey! I . . . got . . . the . . . ring," she says, waving her left hand in my face while trying to catch her breath from the impromptu workout. She swallows hard, takes another breath, and then starts in again. "You said to make marriage a requirement and tell him if he wanted to continue our relationship he needed to give me a ring. I did what you said to do and I got it, Steve Harvey. I got my ring!"

I hear stories like hers practically every day: some women send me letters, telling me they wish they'd had my first book, *Act Like a Lady, Think Like a Man*, on their bookshelves when they were wasting time with a good-for-nothing guy; some women e-mail me stories about how they would have better recognized the guy worth holding on to if they had known in advance what motivates men, which I shared in that book; still others call into *The Steve Harvey Morning Show* or show up to my book signings, relationship panels, and television appearances, or send questions to my online dating site, thanking me for the insight and vowing to keep my advice in mind as they look for, get into, and forge relationships with the opposite sex. With more than two million books sold worldwide and translated into a myriad of languages in over thirty different countries, I'm proud to know that which I spoke about so passionately in *Act Like a Lady, Think Like a Man* was digested, considered, discussed, and ultimately applauded all around the world. I'm also grateful for the doors it opened for me. I have been labeled a relationship expert on a national morning show and in one of the most well-read and respected women's magazines in the world (though I will maintain that I am merely an expert on the mind-set of men in terms of how we think and why we do what we do).

I'll be honest. I did not see this coming. When I set out to write my first book, I did it only intending to share with women who send in questions to the "Strawberry Letter" segment of my radio program and show up to my comedy shows nodding in agreement about my observations on love and relationships, a no-holds-barred guide to understanding what men think about love, sex, dating, and marriage. My sole hope was that it would help women get beyond the myths, stereotypes, and general chatter that puts a stranglehold on the way they conduct themselves in relationships with us; my intention was to inform them about who we really are and what it takes to win in love with us when playing the "dating game."

My intentions were pure: I care deeply about these things because I am a husband, a son, a radio personality who speaks to millions of women daily via my radio show, and, most important of all, the father of four girls—beautiful young women who deserve good men who will love them, respect them, and treat them the way they want to be loved, respected, and treated.

What I found, though, was that *Act Like a Lady, Think Like a Man* simply wasn't enough. As I hosted relationship seminars across the country, I discovered that no matter how thoroughly I thought I'd explained what motivates men, women still had innumerable questions about why we men act and react the way we do in various romantic situations. If I told a group of women that men are driven solely by what they do for a living, how much they make, and who they are, women wanted to know why stability is more important to men than falling in love. If I said men show their love by providing for, professing to, and protecting their significant other, my audience wanted to know why men can't love the way women love—by leading with their hearts. For every question I answered in the chapter, "Quick Answers to the Questions You've Always Wanted to Ask"—from "What do men find sexy?" and "Do you mind if your woman doesn't work?" to "Are men okay with their women having male friends?" and "Is getting on his mom's side important?"—there were fifty more topics I hadn't addressed.

There was also quite a bit of dissension. Some questioned why I counseled women to hold off sleeping with a man for at least ninety days while she investigated his intentions. Some argued that if they dared institute standards and requirements and tell men up front they were looking for serious relationships, they would run off guys who might be interested in them; others questioned whether I, a twice-divorced comedian, am qualified to give advice to women on how to have a long-term successful relationship.

All of these questions, observations, reservations, and demands for clarification and more answers reminded me that women are absolutely the most inquisitive creatures God has created; and no matter how many ways I explain something to my wife, my daughters, my female friends and colleagues, and especially my *Act Like a Lady, Think Like a Man* readers, women are simply going to want to hear the answers more ways than my first book had to offer, and no matter how often I or any other man says they should maybe think and act a little differently in their dealings with men, they're hesitant. Part of this is because other women, mothers, aunts, older female relatives, girlfriends, and (mostly female) editors of women's magazines have been the ones primarily to guide and influence the way women conduct themselves in relationships with men. Rare are the times when men offer up their thoughts on dating and commitment, much less tell women how to make a relationship work. Consequently, when a man does speak up and out on the subject, it often seems to go against all of the advice women have previously received. So I understand some women's hesitancy to embrace the tactical advice I offered up—I get the fear it may have induced.

That's to say that your questions, concerns, complaints, and shouts registered with me—let me know that I needed to go deeper into my explanations about why men do the things that we do so that women could get an even broader understanding of how to either find the man of their dreams or tighten the relationships they're already in, and find satisfaction in their own strength, courage, power, and wisdom.

This time around, I get to the bottom of: why men never seem to do what you want them to do when you want them to do it; how to get the most out of your men sexually; and what men think about dating from decade to decade, from ages twenty on up. I also give a more in-depth visit to both the most popular and the more controversial topics sparked by discussions surrounding *Act Like a Lady, Think Like a Man*, including: what men really think about the long-held notion that we're intimidated by strong, independent women; creative ways to get a man to keep honoring your standards and requirements; learning how to ask men the right questions to get their truthful answers; and tested ways to get a real man to commit to you.

My hope is that when you finish reading this book and really think about the information I'm sharing with you, you'll have an even more informed understanding of men, and certainly an appreciation for how incredibly simple we are. We come at every situation from the same angle, using the same principles, seldom deviating. There really is no use applying your thought process to the relationship equation or expecting your man to adopt your logic when it comes to dating and mating; you can't, after all, change men. I've had countless women ask me, "Steve, when are you going to write a book telling men what they should be doing?" Well, there is no lecture I can give, no panel I can sit on, no television roundtable I can host that will ever make a man pick up a relationship book and dig deep into it. He's simply not going to read it. I can bet you my bottom dollar that even if I were to give this book away, I could count on one hand the number of men likely to pick up a book about how to better get along with women. First off, a man would never allow another man to tell him what he should be doing in his own house with his own woman. Second, I can guarantee you he definitely doesn't want to hear Steve Harvey telling him what to do, not after I gave away the playbook in *Act Like a Lady, Think Like a Man*, and especially after I divulge all of men's relationship secrets here.

Mostly, though, I hope that the women who do choose to read this book find the courage to go against their widely held views on relationships and simply think about and put into practical use the advice I'm giving them in these pages. I understand it's hard to swim in unchartered waters—that it's scary, even. But I encourage you to open your mind and lose the fear. After all, the biggest cause of failure is the fear of failure. If you truly want to change your relationship fortune, why not give change a try? If what you've done up to now hasn't worked, why not try to implement what I've laid out for you in both this book and *Act Like a Lady, Think Like a Man*? Step out—be a risk taker; I'm not telling you to go rock climbing without a safety harness; I'm not saying to go skydiving without a parachute; and I'm not telling you to chain yourself up, submerge yourself in a tank full of water, and try to escape. I'm just asking you to consider thinking about relationships in a different way, based on all of the truths you'll find out about men in the pages of my books.

My sincere hope is that you'll use this information to empower yourself—to recognize that you hold the key to a successful relationship. I understand that many women don't quite care to embrace the idea that the burden of getting the union they want rests squarely on their shoulders, but it is what it is. You've been blessed with this tremendous skill set that we men do not possess, and it is those skills that you absolutely, unequivocally have to employ to get what you want.

Change your approach, take back your power, and hold your chin up while you're working on getting the love you deserve. Do this, and you'll have very little to lose, but a whole lot more to gain.

# PART I

## Understanding Men

# 1

## THE MAKING OF A MAN

I didn't have any business being married at twenty-four.

Yes, I believed wholeheartedly in the idea of marriage; after all, my parents had been married for sixty-four years before my mother passed away. And I had every intention of duplicating what they had: a stable relationship in a home filled with love, strength, perseverance, and wisdom. It was all I knew to do. So it made all the sense in the world to give a ring to the woman I loved and say, "I do."

And that was where the problem began.

In the weeks leading up to my marriage, I didn't have a steady paycheck to support my soon-to-be wife. In my heart of hearts, I knew this wasn't right. I'd even said as much to my mother; I told her I was going to call off the wedding because I wasn't working and it didn't feel right. My mother, being a woman who wanted to see her child married and knew how devastating it would have been to my fiancée to call off her dream wedding, talked me out of canceling the big day. Invitations had been sent out. People were looking for the show. Who was I to rain on this festive parade?

Years later, my mother apologized and admitted she would never have talked me into getting married if she'd known how unprepared I was to be a good husband. By then, we were able to put our finger on what was missing—what was dooming my first marriage even before the spit on the stamps we put on those invitations was dry: I didn't know who I was, what I would do with my life, and how much I was going to make doing it. As I explained in *Act Like a Lady, Think Like a Man*, everything a man does is filtered through his title (who he is), how he gets that title (what he does), and the reward he gets for the effort (how much he makes). These are the three things every man has to achieve before he feels like he's truly fulfilling his destiny as a man, and if any one of those things is missing, he will be much too busy trying to find it to focus on you. He won't have it in him to settle down, have children, or build a life with anyone.

In my first marriage, I didn't have these things lined up by any stretch. I had dropped out of college and went to work at Ford Motor Company. Later I was laid off and didn't get a job until a month after we married. It was a way to make some cash, but I knew it wasn't what I wanted out of life—that it wasn't my calling. And I was frustrated by it. How could I get a wife to buy into me and my plans for the future when even I wasn't enthused by them myself? How could she know me if I didn't know myself? How could she benefit from what I did and how much I made if I wasn't doing or making anything? I was frustrated, our financial outlook was in shambles, and we were always at it—always fighting about something.

Because I wasn't a man.

Sure, she'd married a member of the male species and I had some good traits. I was kind and trusting; I was a very good protector; and I made no qualms about professing to anybody coming and going that she was mine and I was hers. And some good, a lot of good, came from our union: my daughters Karli and Brandi and my son Steve. But I wasn't fully a man. And it cost us.

I wish my father would have warned me, would have sat me down and schooled me on the particulars of marriage. Perhaps he could've told me that a time comes when one needs to cut out all the foolishness—the screwing up in school, the fooling around with a bunch of different women. I wish he would've told me that if I didn't stop acting foolish by a certain age, there would be a cost associated with my lack of focus, with deferring my dreams of being an entertainer. Had he done so, a lot of pain would have been spared for everyone all around. He didn't share with me his thoughts on when a boy needs to focus on maturing into a man. He didn't tell me, "Steve, listen: you got a couple years to date a few women while you figure this thing out, and once you decide who you are, what you want to do, and how you want to make your money, go get a partner who can help you accomplish these things."

That would have been a great lesson for my father to teach his son. But this isn't the way of men.

We are neither the greatest communicators nor sharers of information. There's no manual that says we should know sometime between ages twenty-five and twenty-seven what we want to do with our lives and by ages twenty-eight through thirty, we should be settling down with a woman who is as committed to helping us achieve our goals and dreams as we are to helping her achieve hers. What we constantly hear, instead, is "You're young—sow your oats, enjoy yourself, have a good time, don't get tied down, don't get serious with any girls." And by the time we finish setting ourselves up financially and convince ourselves we're ready to settle down, we've fumbled through countless "relationships," leaving women by the wayside, some of them shattered and bitter because we thought it more important to add a notch to our player belts than to act honorably. We've gone for that gold star some men award each other when they have more than one woman at a time. And for *your* trouble? We get pats on the back—told over and over again that this is what we're supposed to do if we're real men.

Men hardly get pats on the back when they get married.

Even more, married men, whether they're happily married or not, are constantly sharing the horrors of marriage with us, forever pointing out that all the freedoms single men enjoy come to a screeching halt when the ol' "ball and chain" gets attached to a man's ankle—that marriage is some kind of death sentence. Indeed, among men, conversations related to the ins and outs of marriage become conversations based on bravado and jokes, rather than the truth, which is that a marriage—one built on love, respect, loyalty, and trust—is the best thing that could ever happen to a man. Hill Harper pointed this out on a relationships roundtable we did together on *Nightline*; Hill, an actor who's written a few outstanding books on communication between men and women, insisted that single men would benefit greatly if married men admitted publicly that behind closed doors, they are saying to themselves and their wives, "Thank God for marriage. Thank God for my family. Thank God somebody supports me and patches me together so I can go to work the next day. This marriage thing is pretty all right."

It is, for sure, the completion of manhood.

And it's high time we started teaching this to our young men early. We need to pull them aside and explain that there comes a time in which they need to cut out the foolishness. Because once we do we can get back to the business of finding one another, falling in love, creating a family, and spending a lifetime supporting and dreaming and growing—together. This is not something a woman can teach; a man who is twenty-two or twenty-three years old cannot have his mother sitting him down and talking to him about what it takes to be a man; she has no idea of the competition level on which we operate, what drives us, and what we face every time we head toward the front door and out into the world—no more than a man can possibly fathom what it means to be a young woman. We love and admire our mothers to death, but they can't walk in our shoes; men and women are much too different, and she will miss the mark—from the simplest things, like how to shake after you pee, to the most complex situations, like how to square off against another man and, without anyone getting hurt in the process, still be able to walk away with your dignity intact.

Of course, I realize that telling women they can't teach boys how to be men isn't helpful; the world is full of single mothers going it alone while the fathers of their children run from the awesome responsibility of raising them. And it seems that many men who commit to their families by staying the course are often psychologically absent, lost as they are in their work. But it's imperative that boys who do not have their fathers around to show them the ropes get acquainted with some positive, smart, strong male role models—an uncle, a counselor, a coach, a teacher, a neighbor—so that they have someone to talk to, and that someone is vested in making sure that our sons learn the most important lessons.

For sure, I've been teaching this to my own sons, Wynton, Jason, and Steve. And that training starts the moment I open my eyes in the morning. Every day, I have my sons wake up the same time as me—no matter what ungodly hour in the morning it is. If I'm hitting the treadmill and weightlifting at 4:30 A.M., so are they. If I'm going into the office at 5:30 A.M. and I'm working by 6:00 A.M., they're dressed and on their way somewhere too. If they've got school or their study workload is a little heavy, they still have to wake up and, before they get themselves ready, text me their plans for the day—what they're working on and what chore they'll be completing before they sit down for breakfast. This is what typical morning texts from my sons look like:

### May 22

7:06 AM (JASON): Soon, I will be an official Harvey Academy graduate. I take one more test next week and then I'm off to make you proud of me. Today I will sweep the front courtyard and study. Love you Dad, talk to you later.

7:10 AM (ME): I'm already proud. Just give me something to brag about. Give your dad some great moments for his twilight years.

7:11 AM (JASON): Yes sir. Looking forward to making that happen.

And when they mess up, I bring the pain, too. Like just this morning, all of them were supposed to be front and center down in our family gym at 4:00 A.M. to do a group workout with me. Hey, if I'm going to wake up and get on my grind before the sun rises so that I can provide their lifestyle, the least they can do is keep me company while I'm doing it. Well, 4:10 A.M. rolls around and I'm well into my workout and all of my sons were still knocked out; when I called Steve's cell phone, he told me they'd all "forgotten" the plan. I sent a text to Jason first, reminding him that just like in the jungle, the gorilla (me) is always on top of his game and the gazelles (my boys) aren't swift or strong enough to keep up:

7:59 AM (ME):  Gorilla Silverback, 2, Gazelles, 0

8:00 AM (JASON): How'd you score two?

8:01 AM (ME):  Gorilla takes what he wants. I get two points.

8:02 AM (JASON): I'm going to take one back this afternoon. Your Bible is in my room—LOL.

8:02 AM (ME): I told Ms. Anna to put it there. Now you can figure out why. Gorilla 3, Gazelles, 0.

8:06 AM (JASON): Dad how do you keep scoring all the time?

8:15 AM (ME): I never stop coming. This is from your insides, your guts, you hear? Your sinew. Your will to win. Your desire to show up and be counted. Your pride. Where is your pride for doing what you said you're going to do? If I didn't do what I said I was going to do, you all wouldn't respect me. My desire to be respected is so great in me that it pushes me to excel. Where is your pride?

I needed them to know that their father is cranking—that while they were sleeping, I was downstairs doing wind sprints and abs, and then at work earning a solid paycheck so that I could pay our bills to ensure we all have a roof over our heads, beds to lie in, and food on the table—a home. For me. For their mother. For them.

For all of us.

And I talk to them—constantly talk to them—about what it takes to be a real man. If more men truly understood what that means, it would really eradicate so many of the negative relationship issues we grapple with—fatherlessness, low marriage rates, divorce. The list goes on. My dad didn't talk to me a lot, but he showed me by example what it means to be a dedicated father and husband, taught me about hard work and the importance of using it to take care of your family; respecting your significant other and requiring your children to do the same; and being the best father you can be to the babies you make. Did I get it right? Not all the time. I failed at two marriages before I found my relationship stride. That is human. But each time, I drew lessons from the darkness—from the failures. And then I vowed not to let them happen again, not only for the sake of my wife and our marriage, but also to be that example to my children—my sons and my daughters—who are watching me and, like I did with my dad, using my example to get clues about how they should treat a love interest, and certainly how they should expect to be treated by that love interest.

Topping that list of traits every man should have is "Do What You Say You're Going to Do." This is the hallmark of manhood. It's how people judge you—how others determine which level of respect they'll give you. We men brag about what we're going to do all the time—"Oh, don't worry man, I got your back," and "No worries, I got you covered," and "I promise you, I'll be there"—but unless those words are backed up by actions, they mean nothing. Not to your boys. Not to your children. Not to your friends. And especially not to women.

Women don't want to hear excuses for why you didn't follow through on a promise you made, especially when it concerns the well-being of their children. But the man who says he's going to protect his lady needs to be ready to do what it takes to make her safe. A man who promises to provide for his lady works hard every day to make a decent enough wage so that she and the family they made together can have what they need, and maybe even a little bit of what they want. A man who promises to love his lady doesn't step out on her or hit her or wear her out emotionally and mentally; instead he loves her the way a woman wants to be loved—by being faithful and respectful and attending to her needs.

Success in doing all these things is based on that simple tenet of manhood: doing what you said you would do. If you're not doing this, then everyone around you has the right to think that you're just a raggedy dude—your woman has the right to say, "Girl, he ain't worth nothing."

I learned this the first time in my life when I was thirty, after I got kicked out of college and lost my job at the factory and my marriage hit rock bottom. I was living out of my car, driving up and down the road to comedy gigs, trying to establish myself as a comedian, and talking to myself all the way, from city to city, town to town, club to club. I wrote all my jokes out loud; I talked about life and how I got myself into the position where I didn't have a home to go back to. When you're by yourself, you can really get some stuff worked out. I once went for three weeks without having anything more than a quick "Hello, how are you?" conversation with other human beings. I mean, I'd walk into a club, find the manager, and he would say, "Thank you for coming, buddy. You're on for twenty minutes, you get one drink at the bar," and then I'd go up there, tell my jokes, then the manager would come over to me after I'd go offstage and say, "Here's your money, sir—great job," I'd get back in my car and do it all over again. If I was only making seventy-five dollars per appearance, I couldn't blow my money on a hotel, and I sure couldn't waste it on phone calls to anybody, so I would stash my cash and stay in the car and wait for my next gig. You try going even two days without talking to somebody. I'll bet you can't do it. But I did that for three weeks and started asking myself some questions and answering those questions too. I found out a lot about myself and recognized that I wasn't being the kind of husband my wife needed me to be or the kind of provider I needed to be for her and the kids and even for myself. Simply put: I wasn't doing what I said I was going to do. And until I did that, I couldn't truly be a man.

I am not the only man who thinks this way. Over and over again while I was on tour with *Act Like a Lady, Think Like a Man*, men stood up and repeated the same ideals and sentiments. I'll never forget one man who made his way to the microphone at one of my events; he was bald, had a stylish beard, a nice blazer, and a white shirt. The women in the room took notice of him; he spoke about how in his last relationship, he was ashamed because he hadn't gotten himself together—hadn't achieved the career and financial status that he wanted to achieve. But, he added, he'd been working on himself and understanding what he was capable of and he was in a good place. "I'm a good guy," he said, "but I'm a helluva man. I don't have all the money in the world, but I got all the traits that make for a good husband. If you need protecting, I got you. If you need money, I don't have much but what I do have, I'll bring it home. I'll give you my last name. I can do most anything with my hands, so if you need something fixed around the house, I got you covered there, too. And I do what I say, and say what I mean." And then he brought it on home: "What I've been missing is the right woman. If I had the right, stabilizing force in my home—the right support system—I would be even better."

That man finally knows what we all eventually come to know: that we have to learn how to be men before we can be anything to anyone who wants to love us—and certainly before we can love them back. But once we get it right? We come to something close to completion, the thing that makes men want to be better, not only for ourselves, but for the people we love. I can't count the many incredible things that have happened to me as a businessman, a provider, a husband, a father, and a man since the right woman came into my life; I've never in my life gotten the kinds of accolades and accomplishments I've achieved since Marjorie and I started our journey together. I've been on *Oprah*, *Ellen*, a correspondent on *Good Morning America*; I've been invited to speak at a church. *A church.* In my life nobody has asked me to be the keynote speaker in a house of the Lord. Ever. These things I've earned come not only from my deciding to do better, but from somebody seeing that there was better in me. People who've known me for years notice it. Hell, I have a picture of myself from 1995 in which I could see it— the physical toll that my lifestyle and choices were taking on my body, from not being the kind of man I needed to be and not having the right woman to complete the cycle of manhood. My face was sagging, I had put on a ton of weight, I just looked done; it was hard to believe I'd been that miserable.

Now I've put my house in order. I cleared my life of all its debris so that when the blessings did come, including first and foremost my relationship with God, my discovery of what makes me happy—success in my career and a strong, loving woman by my side—I could receive those blessings and start doing right.

And I'm passing that message on to my sons so that they know the secret too: learn how to be a man first. Then find the right woman who can bring out the best in you—make you better. Marriage is not a death sentence. It's a completion.

My sons.

Steve and Jason passed those tests and earned the right to apply to college this past spring. With them, we're going to build a tradition. I was the first one in my family to go to college, but I flunked out. But my sons got accepted into More-house. When they got their letters, I sat in the chair in my office and cried; my sons are going to a prestigious college with a rich and proud legacy, and I couldn't be more pleased. When Jason saw me, he got a quizzical look on his face and asked me why I was upset, what they'd done to make me react in that way.

"You don't even know what this means for me, son," I said simply. "I'm not turning out convicts, there are no babies popping out of the woodwork, and the two of you are going to Morehouse. Give me a moment to celebrate getting it right. This isn't about you."

I recognize my job isn't over—that Jason and Wynton and Steve have quite a ways to go before they are full-on men. But they're on their way.

And I pray that they take the lessons I'm teaching them, and the lessons they'll learn along the way, and make quick work of being the kind of men capable of making someone— themselves and their intendeds—happy. That said, will they make mistakes? Yes. But my job is to limit them.

# 2

## DATING BY THE DECADES

### A Guide to How Men Feel About Relationships in Their Twenties, Thirties, Forties, Fifties, and Beyond

I took my daughter Lori to lunch recently—just me and her, one on one—and I'm not going to lie: I was a little bit more than concerned. It was, after all, the first occasion we'd spent any quality time with each other without her mother, Marjorie, there to quarterback the flow of conversation. I mean, when I take my sons to lunch, the fellowship is pretty low-key; I say, "Find yourself something to eat, man," they order, and we eat. Everybody pushes back from the table happy and satisfied. But the idea of sitting in a restaurant alone with Lori made me come to terms with a couple of things, namely that I haven't a clue what thirteen-year-old girls like, care about, or have on their minds.

But I got a lesson that day.

"So, Daddy, when can I start dating?"

In my head, I was screaming, "Who in the hell is this big-headed boy trying to take you out? You're thirteen—a baby! I'll kill him with my bare hands!" In real time, though, all I could manage was a slow count to ten, some swallows, and a couple of blinks. Finally, when I was sure I would neither shake nor stutter, I dove in.

"How old do you think you should be?" I asked innocently.

"Oh, maybe fourteen or something like that," she said.

I swallowed hard. Again.

"I'm sorry, sweetheart, but nobody can come by the house for you when you're fourteen to take you out. That's way too young."

"Well, my friend Cat dates older guys," she said matter-of-factly.

Of course, in my mind, I had a vision of myself sharpening knives and loading guns and yelling from the front stoop in a housecoat and slippers that anybody named Cat should be forewarned not to so much as step on our block trying to corrupt my baby girl. Little fast butt. Out loud, though, I kept my remarks as calm and measured as I could muster.

"When you say 'older guys,'" I asked politely, "what do you mean?"

"She likes guys who are, like, fifteen or sixteen years old," she said.

I blinked a couple of times and did a few more hard swallows. "Well, baby," I said between sips of ice water. "We'll cross that bridge when we get there."

By lunch's end, I was real clear on this one thing: Lori is not a little girl anymore, and we are in the middle stages of that dance—the delicate tug-of-war between age-appropriate attraction to the opposite sex and all-out boy craziness. I now understand that our conversation didn't mark the first time my daughter's thought about boys and dating and even marriage; if she's anything like every other little girl on the planet, she's considered down to the most minute details what her husband-to-be would look like, what kind of wedding they'll have, where the wedding will be, what kind of material her wedding dress will be made of, and whether she'll smush the wedding cake in her new husband's face. She's probably considered, too, how many kids she wants to have with this dream husband of hers, what their names will be, and whether she'll hyphenate her last name with his.

You know I'm right. This is what girls do; they dream about the Happily Ever After—the wedding, the kids, the married life. Everything they watch—from their Disney movies to their tween television shows to popular music, magazines, and other cultural bellwethers—tells them that while it's okay to be independent, smart, and strong, it should be their priority to meet, get, and keep a husband. And the moment the biological clock starts ticking, whoa! Finding a man to settle down with and have babies becomes quite the priority.

Rest assured, it doesn't work this way for little boys. Ever. There's not a man I know who's sat around dreaming about his wedding day. He may dream of certain women—more specifically, what he'd like to do with them—but trust me when I tell you this: boys and men don't care about marriage the way women do, and we certainly don't sit around fantasizing about it or worrying about biological clocks. Indeed, the way we look at relationships is so far the opposite of the way women see it that it's a wonder, at all, that we even figure out how to be together.

But we do. It just takes a little while for the two of us to get on the same page.

To help you understand why, I thought it only fair to give a decade-by-decade breakdown of what's on the minds of men as it relates to relationships—a guide, of sorts, that will go a long way in showing women what it takes for a man to get into a marriage state of mind.

## A MAN IN HIS TWENTIES . . .

Is just starting to discover the cornerstones of manhood—who he is, what he does, and how much he makes. He's deciding whether to go to college or not, whether to pick up a trade or not, whether to go to grad school or get a master's, or not, and none of his decisions, at least in his early twenties, will help him come to any real conclusions about his future, himself, or his direction in life. Basically, he's using this decade to figure himself out—to work out the kinks before he settles down to the awesome responsibility of being a husband, a father, a homeowner—a man who is responsible for the well-being of not just himself, but other people he loves. In most cases, you simply cannot expect that he'll be ready to provide financial stability and family direction for you when he's still trying to figure out how to make money, get solidified in his career, and make it on his own.

By his midtwenties, he's going to be looking around in the workforce and noticing other men who are homeowners, have cars, and are taking care of families, and his financial clock is going to start revving up. It ticks as loudly as a woman's biological clock does; we hear the calling to start proving we've got the who we are, what we do, and how much we make in order to prove that we are truly men. This isn't nearly as important in the college years because money isn't really all that relevant; everybody there is broke and making their mark by becoming members of social organizations, playing sports, joining fraternities, and being a part of the fabric of campus life. But when he hits age twenty-seven or twenty-eight and he starts seeing his boys drive up to the bar in the fancy car and step out in the fancy suit and whip out a business card featuring both his name and an impressive title in raised lettering, a man in his late twenties is going to want a piece of that action—a fancy car, title, and money of his own. This is critical to him, and nowhere in the playbook is marriage a part of the moves he feels he needs to make to get to where he's trying to go financially and careerwise.

In fact, he may discover on his journey toward figuring out just who he is that he's not responsible enough, yet, for a committed relationship. Or he may have practically every man around him—from his father and brothers to coworkers and friends—telling him that he needs to play the field and put off for as long as possible settling down with one woman. We simply don't preach to our sons the virtues of fatherhood and family—don't tell them that there is a cutoff date for the foolishness and that creating a lasting relationship with one woman is necessary to complete him as a man. He is being driven solely by his financial clock at the same time your biological clock is most likely driving you, and trust me when I tell you, the alarm on his clock isn't set to remind him that it's time to make babies.

## What This Means for Your Relationship

Sure, there are examples of men who can get their careers together, make an adequate amount of money, and be happy enough with their station in life to settle down at this age, but it's more likely that a man at this stage is not going to take any relationships with the opposite sex all that seriously. You can determine whether he has potential, though. The key here is remembering that the word *potential* implies he's capable of taking action. A man who has potential isn't sitting on the couch; he's got a firm plan for what he wants to do with his life and is on his way to being what he says he wants to be. He's got a short-term plan—maybe it includes school or earning enough money to start a company that he's thought through and for which he's created a business plan. And he's got a long-term plan—one that cements how his goal will play out in the future. If he's got no plan, can't articulate his future, and doesn't appear to be working toward any goals, this isn't the guy you want to hang on to.

You also have every right to study what kind of man he's shaping up to be—whether he is respectful, courteous, treats you the way you want to be treated, and is a law-abiding citizen. You deserve to know, too, whether he has hopes and dreams and a sound relationship with God. If he has children, you should be investigating for yourself what kind of man he is to his children and the relationship he has with his kids' mother. You should also be clear that he wants to be in a monogamous relationship and be able to trust that he's acting like he's in one when he's around you. All of these things are an indication of what kind of husband he'll end up being when he is ready to settle down. It's like my coach used to tell me: you're going to play the game the way you practice it. If he's not monogamous while dating you, and his heart isn't morally into doing right by women, what's going to be different when you get married? The only thing that changes after the ceremony is the third finger on your left hand. Everything else? Stays the same. So it will be up to you to be clear about what you require to feel mentally and emotionally satisfied that the man you're with can fulfill those requirements.

Let me be very clear: you have every right to sit this man down and explain what you want as you round the corner and head toward age thirty, telling him that what you accepted in college at age twenty-one is wholly different from what you'll tolerate as a twenty-seven-year-old woman whose body has a limited time span in which to produce babies. It was fine to date, go to parties together, and hold hands out in the quad when you were in college, but he has to respect the fact that your biological clock is ticking and that he should either sign on to the commitment or move on so that you can focus your energy on a man who can give you what you're looking for. Don't be scared: sit him down and say, "Look, I'm twenty-eight and I am looking for a mate right now because I would love to start having children when I'm about thirty-two. I don't want to be thirty-eight having or trying to have my first child, so I'm focused on finding the guy that's right for me." Ask him how old he wants to be when his child, maybe a son, is old enough to toss a football around with him, and remind him that he doesn't want to be that father who's too old to take his teenage son to the hole or chase after his fly ball. I guarantee you that it'll be something he won't have thought about before, because young men don't sit around thinking about such things. Women think about this constantly, and it's okay to let him know that he needs to pick up the pace. The man who truly wants you will accelerate for you; he will pick up the pace and walk in lockstep with you. You can't change him—by his late twenties, he will have solidified who he is as a man. But you can bring out his better qualities. He will be what you want him to be if he knows what will make you happy.

## A MAN IN HIS THIRTIES . . .

Is beginning to solidify himself in his career, is starting to make the kind of money he's wanted to make, and is achieving at least some of the goals he laid out in his master life plan. And once he starts measuring his life and the things he wants to accomplish in it, he starts thinking about settling down. This march toward commitment is boosted by the idealized visions he'll start having about fatherhood: every man will start kicking around the image of himself having a son who dotes on him, wants to be like him, and is a great athlete. He'll dream about teaching his son all the sports he grew up playing, and he'll want to be able to play those sports with his son as he gets better at them, so he'll start realizing that the longer he waits, the less likely his idealized vision of fatherhood will be realized. The question we all ask ourselves in our thirties is, "How old am I going to be when my boy is sixteen?" We still want to be a formidable physical presence in our teenage son's mind, and to compete with him in sports. The last thing we want to be is an old, feeble dad. And so we'll start recognizing that the days are numbered for us to make that ideal scenario a reality—that as we get into our midthirties and beyond, we have less of a chance to play with our boys. Consequently, we'll start thinking seriously about making some babies.

Men in their thirties also start accepting the inevitable—that all of the running around and the chasing we did in our twenties feels like "been there, done that" in our thirties. We become more okay with the idea that our dating days could end one day soon because we feel like we've sampled much of what's out there and the thrill of the hunt isn't all that exciting anymore. The games get old. That's not to say that a man is not excited by a beautiful woman like he was in his twenties or that he's not aroused by hot and sexy women. But after he's gone through a number of relationships and he starts seeing the patterns, he gets real clear on the fact that being with a woman is not going to be all hot and fabulous all the time. So he'll become more open to the idea that if he meets the right person who comes with the least amount of drama and can add support, loyalty, and fun to his life, then he'll accept moving toward commitment. In other words, he'll recognize that he can't play forever, that a grown man has to stop showing up at the club at some point. (This becomes all the more clear the night he goes to the club and he's surrounded by girls who were still in elementary school when he graduated from college. That's a cold reality check.)

Of course, a lot of this is dependent on the age in which a man becomes, in his mind, successful. If he becomes successful in his late twenties, he may be more likely to move toward commitment when he hits his early thirties. By then, he'll feel like he's in good enough financial standing that he doesn't have to kill himself anymore in the workplace with the crazy hours, the networking, and the climbing the ladder. But if it takes him a little longer to become successful, he'll be resistant to the idea of settling down. He'll still be looking at what everyone else has and measuring himself against them—his friends from college who are more successful and making more money than he is, and the ones who aren't doing as well as he. If, on the other hand, he's got it together, or feels like he's close enough to where he wants to be, he'll start warming up to the idea of long-term commitment.

You should note that because a lot of his focus is on making sure he's successful, a man in his thirties will be less concerned about a woman's accomplishments. He won't really care how many degrees you have, and won't be impressed by them, especially if the way you present them, your salary, and your career feels like you're trying to compete with him or suggest that you don't need him to be happy. That's not to say he won't be attracted to an intelligent, successful woman; he just likely won't care about finding his financial match.

## What This Means for Your Relationship

The most important thing you should know about men in their thirties is that you should expect commitment from him, in whatever form you need it. If you're not living together but you're dating exclusively, or you're sharing an apartment and bills, you have every right to expect that he is working toward a long-term relationship with you.

To gauge his level of commitment, start by asking him about family. It's the best way to get a man to think out loud about the future. Ease into the conversation by asking about the numbers: "What do you think your family will look like?" you can ask. "Do you want one kid? Three? Seven?" You might ask, too, about his home life—"Did you get along with your dad? How about your mom? What parenting traits do you think you'd bring with you to fatherhood? Which ones would you do without?" Each of these answers, when you delve deeper into them (I show you how to do this in Chapter 6, "Let's Stop the Games: Asking Men the *Right* Questions to Get the *Real* Answers"), helps you get to the bottom of where this man's head is at when it comes to love, marriage, and family. Asking him about his relationship with his own father could lead not only to a discussion about whether he wants to be a dad, but also what kind of father he sees himself being and the traits he's looking for in the potential mother of his children. All of this is vital information for you as you consider whether he's the right guy to make babies with, and it gives you insight into whether this man is a good fit for you.

You're going to need to pay very close attention, too, to where he is in his career. If he seems unsatisfied and still hustling to put his plan into place, then it's more likely that he's not going to want to commit. You'll be able to tell where a man stands by watching how much time he spends outside of work on hobbies, with friends, playing ball—enjoying more leisure. This tells you that he has time—that he's not all about the job twenty-four hours a day, seven days a week and can find contentment in other things.

Keep in mind that we're talking about ambitious guys here, not the guy who's never been on his grind and avoids hard work or sits around waiting for things to happen for him, or the guy who is still on the grind. Those guys may not wholeheartedly embrace commitment because they're still searching for who they are, what they do, and how much they make, which means they will be too busy accomplishing their career goals to the exclusion of everything else.

Still, the ability to get the commitment from the man who's ready, willing, and able to give you what you want lies with you. You have to be willing to walk away if the commitment you expect isn't forthcoming. There are countless women who've dated a man, fallen for him, given him the cookie, and expected him to return her love and devotion with commitment, only for him to reveal after years of hanging on that he has no interest in marriage. You have to stop waiting to find out if he's willing to commit and ask up front: "Do you ever want to be married?" He might say he's not ready, but you have to push for more information. Ask him when he sees himself getting married—if it'll happen in a year, two, or three. If he comes back with "I'm not the marrying type" or claims he's not looking to get married "anytime soon," don't walk, run away. Let him know that you have every intention of being married in a certain time frame and if he doesn't want to be a part of it, you have to move on. This will be hard for you, I understand; all too many of you fear he will walk away and you will have a hell of a time finding someone else to sign on for a committed relationship. But I've said it before, and I'll say it again: the man you're leaving is not the last man standing. Move on. You made a mistake with that guy, but it's okay. Cut your losses and go find the man you deserve and who wants you back.

## A MAN IN HIS FORTIES . . .

Is feeling good about his station in life and is entering his prime, especially if he's a husband and a father. He loves his accomplishments and he's making money, but at the end of the day, if he has a home to go to, that's major. It completes his journey to manhood. No matter how famous he is, no matter how well he's done for himself, nothing beats coming home to the arms of the people he loves most; his kids are glad to see him, he's the hero all the time. He reveres the title "Daddy." And he's happy that there is a woman who loves him and supports him and makes him feel like he's valued. That's a proud moment for a man, especially when he's old enough to understand the importance of it. By forty, a man wants to feel like he's a stand-up guy who does what he says he's going to do, is respected, has himself together, and can be counted on by his family to be a man. Some struggle with this, but it all comes into focus when he becomes a husband and father. It's a settling moment, and it brings out the best in a man because it pulls out all the love he has to muster: he's going to work hard to make sure his family is provided for; he's going to be proud to announce his wife as his lady and tell everybody about his kids; and he's going to protect his family with the might of the angels.

If he's single, he's single for a reason. He may be unlucky in love. Or he may have signed up for life-altering jobs that made it hard for him to settle down—like working abroad or joining the military. Or he might just be that odd guy who's resistant to the idea of marriage and kids, even after all these years—a bona fide commitment-phobe. Whatever the cause, unless he's a divorcé, he's resigned himself to the fact that the traditional family—a wife and kids—may not happen for him (or he's decided he doesn't want to be bothered with it at all), and so he becomes comfortable with the idea of a life alone. If he has nieces and nephews or close friends with children, he's perfectly happy doting on them, and he doesn't feel as if his life is missing anything; he's just as satisfied with this arrangement as all the women out there who don't think their lives are horrible failures if they don't have kids and a ring. Life is about comfort for them; they are financially comfortable, have established comfortable routines, and have comfortable lifestyles. And they're not necessarily lonely because they put themselves in situations where the female company they keep isn't disruptive to their day-to-day lives. This is a nice way of saying it's going to take a lot for someone to come along and jar the overall sense of ease to which the single, fortysomething man has grown accustomed. In his mind, he's thinking that commitment will disrupt his perfectly stable, doable, enjoyable arrangement—one in which he does what he wants, when he wants to, without having to be accountable for anything or anyone but himself.

Now, this doesn't mean that the fortysomething man is not susceptible to meeting a woman who rocks his world—who makes him think he can't live without her. It's just that he's mastered the art of companionship and isn't necessarily as driven to hunt for women and meaningless sex as he was in his twenties and thirties. As a man gets older, he doesn't need sex as much, and he's already had relationships with a wide and diverse group of women, so the hunting he did in his younger days slows down. He's not trying to be in the clubs or at the sports bars looking for the young, hot thing. He's going to be more attracted to somebody he can talk to, whom he can have a nice meal with and go out to events, concerts, and other recreational events with; who fulfills his sexual needs; and who, like him, doesn't feel any pressure to make the relationship any more than what it is. This is comfortable for him; it's what all men want—comfort, peace, and companionship—and the forty-year-old single guy is going to have this in abundance. He's arranged it this way.

Of course, if he's a fortysomething divorcé, he's likely alone because he's wary, but more prone to the hunt because he's back out on the dating scene and reacquainting himself with all the women he had to walk by with blinders on while he was married for the last decade. Now that he can actually sample without repercussions, he's going to want to play for a minute. It may take him a few years before he's even thinking about committing to anybody again, especially if he's newly divorced and still has some very strong and complicated emotions about his ex. Still, it's true what they say about a man who has been married before: if he committed to someone once, he's certainly not scared of it and would be open to doing it again. He won't necessarily romanticize it, but he will remember how wonderful it can be and won't completely be opposed to the idea of marriage after he's gotten the playing out of his system.

## What This Means for Your Relationship

You're going to have to be more thoughtful about how to find a forty-year-old single man and especially how to approach him. He's been there, done that, and he's not going to be fooled by nice bodies, batting eyelashes, and coy behavior. Sure, he knows how to go find some hot twentysomething who perhaps he'd be willing to spend a couple nights with, but mostly, he's done that so many times it has very little interest for him; he knows that the chances are high that the younger women haven't done anything, haven't been anywhere, and haven't yet had the adult experiences he's had. Instead, he's going to need and want someone who's got something going on, and who is interesting and especially interested in the things he's built into his life to make it comfortable.

This means, too, that you're going to have to be a little bit more creative in trying to find him. He's not going to be found in the club or in the gym or the sports bars—typical places where the opposite sex meets when they're young, hot, and fresh. You're going to find this guy at a jazz club, actually listening to the music, or at sporting events, enjoying the game, or on the golf and tennis courts or in the football league. As a single man, he can indulge in these kinds of entertainment and sporting hobbies because there's no wife telling him that he's being indulgent and selfish for structuring a lifestyle that's enjoyable to him.

Know that hopping into a relationship with a divorced fortysomething man may be tricky if his divorce is new. There may be a lot of ways he sees his ex's face in yours and runs in the other direction. If he's been divorced less than two years, you should prepare yourself for some bedroom play and not much else; he's probably going to want to keep it moving, no matter how fabulous you are. That's because forty-year-olds don't believe the hype. In his twenties, he believed anything a woman told him, and in his thirties, he got a little more skeptical. But in his forties, he doesn't believe much of anything women tell him. They're all fabulous cooks who love to keep a clean house by day and dress in lingerie every night; not a one of them dare leave the house without makeup on; they love sex, are avid basketball and football fans, and love the smell of cigar smoke—until, that is, they get into a relationship and the pretty packaging falls off. As a man who was married before, he already knows there are very striking similarities in the way women in relationships respond to pressure, stress, and challenges, and so when life comes along and creates difficulties for them, he knows there's a good chance that he may wind up back in the same place he was with the woman he divorced. So you're not going to lure him by telling him how wonderful being with you is; he may not believe you. You'll have to show him, rather than tell him. If he takes you out on the golf course and you look like you're having fun, or he takes you to the sports bar and you argue with the most avid fan about the merits of the Lakers' triangle offense, or if you can discuss the beauty of a Coltrane versus Miles Davis classic solo, then he may start believing that you have a lot of the same interests as he does and that you're a unique one-of-a-kind catch.

Once he's moved on from the hurt of the divorce and he starts getting lonely, he'll realize that sex with a forty-year-old does, in fact, have the potential to be a lot more interesting than sex with a twenty-five-year-old; he's well aware that physical perfection isn't always what it's cracked up to be and he's going to start wanting more companionship—the woman who's comfortable with her station in life and his, too.

## A MAN IN HIS FIFTIES AND BEYOND . . .

Is working desperately to solidify his legacy. Simply put: he's looking at the tape and trying to figure out how to set up his family for when he's done working or after he's gone from this earth. He's thinking more in terms of security than he ever has before, even as he's looking forward to emptying his nest—

sending the kids off to college or to start their new lives on their own so that he can enjoy his significant other in ways he hasn't since the two of them had children. He's more content in his newfound peace with his lady and is settled into the life he's built, but still worries about protecting his family—not with brute force, but by making sure they can survive without him.

This mind-set is boosted by his ever-changing body. He starts to worry about it because it's in his fifties that his body starts to betray him. His blood pressure increases, his cholesterol levels increase, his prostate gives him problems, and there are aches and pains that he's never felt before. All of this makes him much more aware of his mortality, and he realizes he has to take better care of himself. This, of course, is much easier for him when there's a woman around. It's a lot harder for a man to live right, eat right, and stay out of trouble if there isn't a female presence there to tap him on the shoulder and remind him why it's better to leave the cheesecake and steak alone and eat more vegetables, get in more exercise, and stay out of trouble for the sake of not only himself, but the ones he loves.

## What This Means for Your Relationship

He's going to be a lot more open to the idea of having a woman around not only to love in the way that a man loves—by protecting, professing, and providing for her—but also because he knows that a fairly sweet, nurturing, caring woman will increase his life expectancy by at least a decade. This will put him in a better position to want to commit to someone, certainly more so than a man in his thirties and even forties. He will basically be looking for someone to grow old with as he faces the other side of the high-paced workforce and begins to imagine what it will be like to do all the things he always wanted to do—travel or spend leisurely, carefree afternoons—with a steady companion who also is happy to finally be settled down and enjoying the rest of her life.

*P*lease understand that these different stages of manhood are not ironclad definitions of men at these different ages; there are always exceptions to the rule. What I've described here is a generalization of what happens in men's lives as they move from decade to decade—things that I've gone through myself, and certainly experiences that friends of mine have shared with me during the course of our friendships. My sincere hope is that you'll use this as a loose guide to understanding just where your man's head may be when it comes to a relationship with you—an understanding that just may help you get the kind of love you want, need, and deserve.

# 3

$\rightarrow$—$\twoheadleftarrow$

# ARE WOMEN INTIMIDATING?

## Myths Versus Facts

As the success of *Act Like a Lady, Think Like a Man* mounted, so too did the fever pitch of television specials, newspaper, and magazine stories questioning why it's so difficult for single women who are intelligent, successful, beautiful, and, by their own accounts near perfect, to so much as find a date, much less a husband. And always, always, the most vocal single women either claimed they were perfectly happy being alone or they laid the blame for their unmarried status squarely in the lap of men: "I'm alone because men are *intimidated* by me."

Sorry, but as the title of this book suggests, I'm going to have to give it to you straight, no chaser and, at my own peril, take one for the team: in the minds and hearts of most men, the notion that a guy is "intimidated by your success" is nothing more than an excuse—a convenient way for some women to rationalize why they're alone. Harsh but true. When we're away from the womenfolk and talking among ourselves out on the golf course or on the basketball court or while enjoying a cigar at the bar, we men give a chuckle, shake our heads, and wonder aloud who told you this madness. Because, nothing, really, could be further from the truth. Men don't mind strong, independent, capable women by any stretch. What we do mind is feeling like we're not needed.

Believe it or not, there is a difference.

Still, this "men are intimidated by me" myth persists, as do others concerning women who are independent, particularly women who are financially or emotionally self-sufficient. So I am addressing these issues with the hope that, if women truly understand the mind-set of a man when he goes mano a mano with a strong, independent, successful woman, we can move the dialogue forward.

## MYTH 1

### Men Don't Like Women Who Talk About Their Material Success

**THE TRUTH:** If you've got a degree or two, a fancy car, a nice place to lay your head at night, and a paycheck that'll make a Fortune 500 CEO drop his jaw in awe, we are happy for you. Yes, you read that right. *Happy.* It doesn't anger us, turn us off, or deliver a crushing blow to our self-esteem and ego if a woman has done well for herself and is living a splendid life.

But if that's the defining element of your life—if this is what you live and die for, and the first thing out of your mouth after you introduce yourself is the year and make of your car, the purchase price on your fancy home, your credit score, followed by the single, strong, independent female creed—"I don't need a man to take care of me!"—then guess what we're going to translate that into? "Your services are not needed here." And we will take our services elsewhere while you climb that corporate ladder alone. Worship alone. Raise your child alone. Shop alone (or with your girlfriends). Take all your vacations alone (or with your girlfriends). Only to return home . . . alone. There's nothing wrong with being alone, mind you. Plenty of women are on their own, content with lives full of good friends and great experiences that don't necessarily involve committed relationships with the opposite sex.

Yet for every woman who says she's just fine by herself, there is a whole host of others who really are unsettled by the idea that they may not find the happily ever after that they thought would be waiting for them once they acquired the career, money, and status they worked so hard to get, and who really do believe with all their hearts that they're alone because men are intimidated by or jealous of their success.

Here is the thing, though: it is already obvious to most men that the majority of women can take care of themselves. If you were raised by parents who were even remotely concerned about your well-being, they likely taught you the importance of getting a solid education, pursuing a good career, and having the wherewithal to take care of yourself, whether a man is in your life or not. Men expect that you followed through on this promise to yourself and are doing all you can to be the best you can be, and we know it's only natural for people, women included, to share things about themselves that they're proud of.

What turns us off is when your personal seams are sewed up so tight we can't see where we can fit in and what role we can play in your life. You leave us no room to be men. As I've said elsewhere here and in *Act Like a Lady, Think Like a Man,* the way a man shows his love for a woman is by providing for her, protecting her, and professing for her—giving her the title of girlfriend, lady, or wife. Now if you tell a man you don't need him to provide for you, you have all the cash you need to cover your bills and your lifestyle, and that you don't need his protection because between your alarm system and Jake, the pit bull, your mansion is safe—then what would make him want to profess his love for you?

Now, I understand that not all women are slinging their degrees and salaries and material gains in men's faces to brag and suggest that they don't need men. There is, too, this pervading idea that women need to list their accomplishments in order to not appear "needy" in men's eyes, so that guys won't think they're being pursued for their money and material wealth. But here's the rub. Everybody needs somebody. And everybody has voids they need filled: they want companionship, a family, someone to help them feel safe, someone to share their dreams with, someone who can be a male role model in their home, someone willing to listen to their problems and maybe even offer up a few suggestions on how to fix them too—even someone for less complicated things, like mowing the lawn, taking care of the car, and dealing with the bills. And you know what? We don't mind if you need us. In fact, it's only a turnoff to men who, for whatever selfish reasons, don't want to fulfill your needs. The man who is genuinely interested in having a solid relationship with you wants to care for you, wants to hold your hand and provide a shoulder that'll help you through the hard times, wants to spend his money making sure you're provided for, wants to make sure no one ever hurts you, wants to be a good father to your children, wants to see you succeed because he knows it's for the greater well-being of the family *and* makes you happy. We have no interest in creating you. We want to come in and complete you.

If you're constantly saying you don't need us, well, maybe you don't.

You don't have to sell yourself short or dumb it down. Of course you can still be proud of your accomplishments and share them with men, too. But how about adding a little truth to the mix. There's nothing wrong with running down your credentials and then following them up with some truth about what you still desire but don't yet have: "I'm really happy with my station in life—I've accomplished a lot. But I'm looking for a man who completes me. I've got myself halfway to where I want to be, but I dream about having a family and a husband who will be my partner in life." Sharing your vision with a man and being clear about what you want in a relationship without devaluing him takes true courage—true strength. A man can sign up for that. A buddy of mine did exactly that when a woman to whom he was attracted made plain to him that she was looking for "the one" to live out the rest of her life with. He met her in a bank; he was the teller, she was the customer— and the chemistry between them was electric. She would give him flirtatious smiles, he would do his best to keep up the small talk so that she would stick around a little while longer. After a few months of flirting with the idea of taking her out, my friend finally did the deed: he asked her out for coffee at a local shop. She happily accepted his invitation and, over coffee and Danish, proceeded to blow him away. He already knew that she was financially set; he was, after all, her banker. But during their meeting, he also learned that she ran her own company, which she'd started after picking up clients and a lot of know-how working for—and becoming wealthy from—a longtime position at a Fortune 500 company. She wasn't bragging—just sharing information about herself. And then she laid out for him exactly what she was looking for: "I'm a good woman, I have a great life and family and friends, but I know, too, that I want a man to love and who loves me back. That would be the ultimate for me." She explained further that at forty-plus years old, she wasn't looking to marry a millionaire; she just wanted a steady, faithful companion with whom she could build a solid life.

This stuck in the back of my friend's mind. He may not have been able to buy her the biggest house on the block or add zeroes to her bank account or be in the position to make decisions that would affect her career, but he could still find room in there to be a man—to provide for her and protect her and have the broad set of shoulders she needed to lean on while they built that life together. It didn't take him long to become the man she needed—the man she was looking for. And after more than a decade together, they're still going strong.

## MYTH 2

### Men Don't Approach Strong Women Because They're Intimidated by Them

**THE TRUTH:** We're not intimidated by strong women. Intimidation is just another word for fear, and although men are afraid of a lot of things, women aren't one of them. You can't kick our behinds, and, short of that, little scares us. If we see you from across the room, we're not counting the zeroes in your bank account, and we sure aren't wondering what your job title and position is at work. We don't care about that. Initially, we don't even care how many kids you have, or what your dreams and goals and ambitions are. We just want to talk to you. But we will only do it if it looks like you won't give us attitude simply for approaching you. Give us some credit; we're way more crafty than you think—believe me when I tell you.

Men are hunters by nature, predators who, if we're not looking for anything serious, will look for the easy kill. The woman who's dressed provocatively, who's a little loud, who's tossing back drinks and dancing suggestively and sending out the signals that she's down for whatever won't have a problem filling up her dance card with a bunch of guys who won't be remotely serious about her. She's going to be the ultimate throwback for the man who's sport fishing, a man who is looking for a woman to use and toss back into the water. She's easy to spot. But we can also spot, just as easily, the woman who has it all, plus attitude to spare—and who isn't afraid to use it.

We're not as stupid as you think we are, I promise you that. We don't just run up on you; we watch you. We watch how you talk to the lady in the cafeteria line at work—how rudely you talk to her, how you don't say "thank you" when she gives you your change and packs up your sandwich. We see who you choose to sit with—how you sit with only a certain type of person, but avoid anyone who doesn't fit into your mold of "success." We sense when you're throwing off that "you're really beneath me, why are you over here" vibe when guys with a certain look head your way. We determine things about you before we walk that long stretch to get to you, before we figure out just the right words we'll say to get you to smile. And if we get the sense that you won't smile, that you're going to give off that "why are you over here" attitude, we're not going to approach you. We're going to conclude that we don't need to deal with you.

If men aren't approaching you, maybe it's not because you're intimidating but because they're too busy focusing on the woman who isn't cold and callous—the one who is smiling and comfortable with herself and appears to be having a good time, even if she is sitting alone.

If a woman looks engaging, we'll engage her. But if she looks like one of those cold women who will meet our advances with hostility and act disinterested when any man even looks in her direction, well, yeah: men aren't going to talk to her. Who needs that hassle? Who *wants* that hassle?

## MYTH 3

### Men Can't Be in Relationships with Women Who Make More Money

**THE TRUTH:** A man who makes less money than you isn't holding it against you. He's taking it out on himself.

First, you must understand that it is possible for men to be in serious relationships with women who bring in more cash. These days, with the economy in flux and men losing their jobs only to leave their women the biggest—and sometimes the sole—breadwinners in the house, there are more examples of unions that fit this bill than ever before. But it is not easy, by any stretch, for a man to swallow that, and it's going to take some serious strategizing to make this work. His difficulty handling the financial imbalance isn't about you—it's about him. He's not intimidated by or mad at you for succeeding; it's more that he's ashamed that he's not growing with you. If he's not moving forward financially or in terms of his status and position, if he's not accomplishing anything special or feels like he's not living up to his promise, as a man, to provide for his family, then he's going to have problems seeing where he fits into the equation, particularly if it involves changes he didn't sign up for.

Say you've gotten a promotion and now you're taking more

phone calls, answering more e-mails, and going on more business trips, whereas he's stuck at the house, trying to keep the kids quiet while you work or taking them to school and picking them up because you're not there to do it as regularly as you used to. If this wasn't something he was doing before, and those changes came along without any discussion or agreement about how familial and household responsibilities will now be divvied up, your man is either going to begrudge his new position or rail against it. For a guy to go from being a workingman all his life to playing Mr. Mom will take a toll on him. When you're going against everything that feels like the natural order of things and you're forced to play a role that falls outside your skill set, without your permission or your partner's acknowledgment of what you're going through, it's a hard pill to swallow. If your man didn't raise his hand and agree to be Mr. Mom, get ready for some degree of rebellion. Some men can make the adjustment, but some can't.

Not, at least, without your help.

This is where it will be important to communicate and be very clear about what it will take to work together to keep the family intact. And this is where your tone will be important. Sit him down and talk to him like the lady you are; acknowledge that the financial dynamic is different and unexpected and unlike any one you've ever handled in your relationships, but that the dynamic between you and him is the one that is most important to you and the two of you have to be willing to do what it takes to make it work. Reiterate to him that you two aren't in some kind of paycheck competition—that the money you're bringing in isn't solely for you, but for the team, the family, and that everyone in the house benefits when the two of you work together to keep the cash flowing, no matter whose faucet is flowing harder. Pump him up—tell him that you still have his name as do the children, and you still consider him, without question, the fearless leader and head of the household. Offer him encouragement, support, and show him appreciation; it'll go a long way in helping him deal.

Sure, there will be some of you who take issue with this, who think that putting him on a pedestal will somehow devalue you. But I ask you this: Isn't your relationship worth it? His feelings? Is it so awful to boost up the man you love? Wouldn't you want him to do the same if the tables were turned?

I'm guessing you would.

He can deal with the changes as long as your attitude and your tone don't devalue his worth. Success outside the home will not translate into success inside your home if you're using your financial upper hand as an excuse to talk to and treat your man like an employee or your child. Men are not inflexible; it's all in the approach.

## MYTH 4

### Men Expect and Want Strong, Independent Women to Lower Their Standards or Get Comfortable Being Alone

THE TRUTH: Men really don't care about what model, make, and specification of a man you prefer; if you're looking for a mate who, like you, has a couple degrees, a high-paying salary in a fast-paced career, a mansion on the hill, and a fancy car to drive you to expensive restaurants, that's your business. It bears no reflection on us, and we applaud you for sticking to your guns about the kind of man you want. But if there aren't a bunch of those guys fitting that specific bill standing around waiting for you, don't go broadcasting from the mountaintops that there aren't any good men around, because there are plenty of "good" men around. What gets our goat is the refusal of strong, independent, extremely picky women to acknowledge that maybe, just maybe, one of the biggest reasons they're alone is because they've severely limited their dating pool by skipping over perfectly good guys for less attainable ones.

To us it's like when we're twelve and we're thinking about what we want to be when we grow up. We tell everybody we want to play center field for the New York Yankees. Even though there are a billion of us who want that job, only a few of us will actually get the job, and at some point, we realize it's probably not going to be us. Consequently, we adjust our expectations and come up with a more reasonable, attainable career goal.

There might be some benefit to applying this logic to dating. If you feel like your MBA, bank account, and baubles make you a contender for center field—the cream-of-the-crop bachelors, the men who are handsome, fit, smart, tall, educated, and rich, in addition to all of the other things you expect from a man— go for it. But if you keep getting passed up for the gig, don't get bitter about it. There's nothing worse or more annoying to a man than the old guy standing around with nothing but a dollar and a dream and his coulda, shoulda, woulda stories about how he'd have been the greatest center fielder the Yankees ever had if someone would have just given him a chance. He's broke and jobless and bitter because he couldn't see the bigger picture—refused to exercise his options.

Men get it: you worked hard to get where you are, and you feel like you need and deserve someone who worked hard in the same way and acquired the same education and status as you did and has similar experiences and goals. But there are a lot of different ways of working hard and striving, and men can't—and won't—tolerate it when women dismiss their idea of success for their narrowly defined way of characterizing accomplishments and achievements. In essence, you're looking for a man who is your financial and educational twin; you're exceptional in a certain kind of way and you want him to be exceptional in a similar vein, which means you're limiting your dating pool to a very small subset of men. This would be fine if men in the subset you're looking in were limiting their dating pool to their economic and educational twin as well. But chances are, they're not, because those aren't the qualities that men tend to prize in a mate. Men look at qualities that draw from a much larger subset—someone who is good-looking, nurturing, kind, smart (enough), stable, noncompetitive, cheerful, fun to be around. Those traits may lead a man to a whole other subset of women who bring something entirely different to the table than you can or would.

What people—men in particular—are saying is that it might be more helpful to you to adjust your priorities and focus on traits that are the hallmark of a true relationship built on a solid foundation. A man who works a blue-collar job, drives a Taurus, and is attractive, family-oriented, respectful, and trustworthy may not ever help you achieve your wildest financial aspirations, but isn't that the kind of guy who brings to the table the standards that will help you build a good relationship and life together? And say the guy driving the Range Rover with a collection of impressive titles and the big salary fits your bill financially and educationally, but he's not trustworthy or honest and is, oh, I don't know, horrible in bed. Would he still fit the bill of the perfect guy?

There are plenty of good men ready, willing, and capable of doing right by you if you let them. And you have every right to weed through them to get to what you want and stand firm until you get it. Just remember that you're the one making the decision to limit your dating pool, and if you end up alone, it's on you. We don't take any pleasure in your being alone, but we're certainly not going to take the blame for it either.

## MYTH 5

### Men Who Date/Marry Independent Women Are Lazy and Just Looking for a Sugar Mama to Take Care of Them

**THE TRUTH:** Sure, a few guys out there take advantage of women with money to burn. That's human nature. But it's not a trait even remotely embraced by men. In fact, this kind of behavior goes against every cell in our being. It's admitting weakness and failure to a woman, and to a man, that's the worst thing in the world. We want women to think of us as strong and capable—especially the women we love. We're raised to believe and internalize the age-old notion that we're supposed to be the protector and the provider; when that's in a man's mind, there's little room for fantasies featuring a financial princess who swoops in and takes responsibility for our subsistence. It's one thing to accept gifts from a woman who likes to give them, but if she's helping a man eat and providing a place for him to lay his head and buying his clothes and making it so he can survive because he can't do it on his own, he's not going to stick around for long. Don't believe me? Why do you think there are so many single-parent families and absentee fathers? Some men leave because they can't take being in the home if they can't provide for their women and children. It's unfortunate that these two things are interconnected, but a man can't see himself being a good father if he can't see himself providing for his family. In our minds and in yours, and the collective mind of society, the two—fatherhood and income—are inextricably linked. So if he's not providing, the last thing he wants is someone—particularly his woman—accusing him of being less than a man. As a result, he'll leave before he signs up to be taken care of by a "sugar mama."

This doesn't, however, mean that men aren't willing to even entertain the offer of help. That you're willing to open your heart and make a personal sacrifice so that we can have something better for ourselves is never lost on us. Indeed, it tells us something about the kind of woman you are—what kind of partner we might expect if we decide to hitch our wagons together. For sure, Marjorie won me over with her willingness to be selfless. She was there when I went from making a lot of money to making absolutely no money. I'd just given up my radio show in Los Angeles, and my TV show, *Steve Harvey's Big*

*Time*, had been canceled; to make matters worse, it was summer, a difficult time for comedy tours, so from June through August, I wasn't going to make money touring. I was also tied up in an asset division case and had moved to New York without any real home in which to settle. Marjorie saw all of this but she didn't say, "You know what? I'm not going to get more involved with you." Instead, this woman, who is extremely strong and independent, who was living in her own home, helping to run her own family's successful business, raising her own kids, and living her own life, offered to open her home to me. She literally took me to her house in Memphis and said, "Steve, we can live here."

As I looked around, I said to myself, "Well, um, this is cute and all." She'd decorated her home beautifully and she's an amazing housekeeper (her home was immaculate), but it was small and there was no gate. I kept trying to explain to her that up until that very moment, after years of struggle, I'd been doing really well professionally and had every intention of doing even better going forward, these setbacks notwithstanding, and that a home without a gate could get really tricky for a celebrity. But none of that mattered to her. She kept telling me, "You don't have to tell me that." She had her own money and her own struggles, but she was riding out the latter and was willing to share her money with me, as long as I came to the table with the things she required: that I act like a father to her children, that I was a faithful husband, that I was a partner with whom she could share her dreams of the future, and that I could make her feel safe.

For her, everything was about family and the quality of her

relationship, which told me where she was in her life and that what she wanted was much bigger than a bank account.

All this myth debunking is meant to help you understand that it's time to let go of the whole notion that the reason strong, independent women can't find men is because we men are afraid of your power. We are not afraid of you. We applaud your success. We're not looking for you to take care of us. We don't have a problem with you making more money. Indeed, we want you to be happy. And we don't revel in your being alone. We do care about attitude, however—your attitude toward material things, your attitude toward others, your attitude toward us when we're down and going through a transition of sorts.

# 4

## EVERY SUGAR DADDY
## AIN'T SWEET

I get why it's so easy to get sucked in.

Here's this guy at your door bearing gifts—say it's the latest Fendi bag, a pair of Christian Louboutins to match the hot, body-skimming dress he laid across your bed last month, or a pair of diamond earrings the size of fists and a matching bangle so sparkly it makes your wrist look like a constellation. Or those gifts might be something much more practical—a check to cover a month's worth of rent for the condo you all spend time in, or a payment for that Chrysler you've been driving around town, or a date in the chair of that stylist you love who sews in your tracks just the way you (and he!) like them or gives you highlights that all the women in the office envy. Hell, he might be bringing something as basic as a bag of groceries or lunch money for the kids.

Whatever the gift, you're happy to receive it, aren't you? Because it keeps money in your pocket and, more important, it makes you feel like this man cares about you—wants you to look good, live comfortably, eat right, and have some of your needs and even some of your wants taken care of. Who wouldn't sign up for that, especially if this guy is bringing these gifts and showing you what appears to be genuine affection?

But you know, back in the day, that guy was referred to as a "sugar daddy." Sugar Daddy is a sweet person who takes care of you like your daddy would—gives you clothes, food, shelter. Delivers it all with sweetness beyond compare, but with expectations no "daddy" would ever expect of his real daughters. The sugar daddy motto: you be sweet to him, and he'll be sweet to you.

These days, a sugar daddy has a different name: sponsor. No matter if you all call this man a "sugar daddy" or a "sponsor," we men simply refer to him as a player and you as a woman willing to prostitute yourself without even realizing it.

Yup, I said it.

Sure, you may be getting some nice things, but honestly, accepting gifts from a guy without getting what you want in return is nothing more than an advanced form of prostitution. See, we men understand this much: there's a "cost"—direct or indirect—associated with sex. We can buy it at the strip club or at a brothel or online, or we can take you to dinner and the movies, pay your rent, buy you some jewelry, send you to get your hair done on our dime, or hand you money. Either way, we fully expect that if we're spending money, we're going to get something in return: sex.

And trust me when I tell you, there is nothing sugary or sweet about giving so much of yourself to a man who, at the end of the day, is giving up so little in return. Oh, it may look like he's giving you the world. Hell, a sugar daddy/sponsor/player will go out of his way to make it seem like he's going all out, just for you. But a sugar daddy who is, in essence, paying for sex will never make any real, long-term sacrifice, will never pursue anything that substantially chips away at his own bottom line. He'll play the game as long as it goes undetected and will not interfere with a relationship that's important to him.

He will not pay your rent if it means he can't pay his.

He will not buy you a car if he doesn't have one for himself.

He will not buy you groceries if his refrigerator isn't full.

He will not take you to the hot party if a woman he cares for more wants to go too.

And he most certainly will not fall in love with you just because you're giving him some tail.

In my line of business, I see this all the time. Men with means—celebrities, athletes, bankers, businessmen—have one, two, three, and even more women on the side, and each one of them will be the proud recipient of a sponsorship package: they might get $2,000 for rent in a luxurious condo, maybe $700 for a car note, $300 for hair and nail appointments, an expensive pair of shoes or a dress every now and again. Tally that up, and those women have gotten something very valuable from their sugar daddies, haven't they? They have a place to live and transportation, and they get to look good from head to toe—all on someone else's dime. But what they're getting from their sponsors is worth nothing more than a dime to a sugar daddy in the scheme of things; if he's making millions, what is that little $3,000 a month costing him? The woman who's getting that sponsorship package is worth very little—the equivalent of a drawerful of cashmere Marcoliani socks, a few fancy Hermès ties, and a pair of expensive cuff links. He might as well be flipping a quarter in her direction.

If you're involved with a sugar daddy or sponsor, you don't even have to ask for that quarter either. The real players always offer to help you with whatever your needs are before they're expressed—we pick it up in conversation, see it with our own two eyes. You pull up in a car that looks like it's on its last leg? A sugar daddy's got a car payment for you or a ride to wherever you need to go. A potential sponsor comes over to your house and sees that all your furniture looks like it came from the 1950s and your two little kids' hand-me-downs date back to the 1970s? Your sponsor is going to be sure to kick you a little cash for some new furniture or take the kids clothes shopping. A sugar daddy goes out with a woman and looks down at her feet and asks what size she wears. Please believe, he's going to make a mental note that she said she wears a size 9, and a few weeks later when she's not thinking about it, he's going to show up with a nice pair of shoes in the perfect size. Those shoes are going to get him a kiss. And when he asks her what size dress she wears, a few weeks later, he's going to trade in a size 10 outfit for a hug and a kiss and maybe a little bit more. The woman hasn't said she wants clothes or a dress or anything else, but she's not turning it down, either. The money and the gifts are bait, and he knows she's biting.

He's going to keep the bait coming, too, because he's investing in her. It's just a slick way of giving her what *she* values—a way to reel her in without sacrificing anything he truly needs or wants. And what kind of return does he get on his investment? Something that no man should be able to buy: her love, her devotion, and her body—three things that are absolutely priceless.

And trust me, a player doesn't have to be rich to offer sponsorship packages. The regular workingman is just as much an expert at investing in a woman as the richest man on the planet. You're short on cash and running out of milk? Here come some groceries, some baby food, and a couple of lollipops for the kids. You a little light on money for the bills? Here comes a couple dollars toward the phone and light bills. Your car's not running right? Here he comes to change the oil or check on the timing belt or change the flat tire. He doesn't have to have a lot of money—he just needs to see a need and fulfill it, at minimal or no cost to himself.

Please understand, there really is a difference between a man who provides and one who is simply investing. As I've said elsewhere in this book, a man who truly loves you will do three things: profess his love for you publicly, protect you by any means necessary, and provide for you, no matter if it means there's nothing left for himself. He will not spend his money on trifling things and come to you with what's left, and he will not selfishly give you a little cut and take the rest for himself. If he's a real man, he will always sacrifice buying something for himself until he's fulfilled his responsibility to provide for you; he will not buy a new set of golf clubs or a nice suit if he knows the kids' tuition is due. He does this because providing for you—even if it means sacrificing what he needs for himself—is fulfilling his role and purpose as a man who is showing his genuine love for his woman.

A man who is buying baubles and trinkets but refuses to give you what you really want—a true, monogamous, loving relationship, however, is simply using you. He's paying your rent and car note, but he's doing it only because he expects something in return, and the moment it starts costing him to keep buying you, he's out. His sponsorship package may make you feel grateful to be with him, but really, you're being played—kept in a holding pattern until he's ready to move on. He's buying your kindness, your sex, your love, your affection—a cool place to chill out and escape whatever problems he's dealing with, like the nagging wife or girlfriend, or the dog-eat-dog competition at work, or the pressure that comes with raising kids with a difficult ex. And while you're letting him spend money on you and giving him your all, you're compromising your requirements and standards and missing out on what most women looking for a sound relationship want in a man—understanding, tenderness, companionship, a man willing to share himself and grow with you and truly sacrifice for you. He reels you in by telling you he's with you because he can find peace in your arms, but *you're* not finding any peace.

A true player knows how to, well, play on your needs; he's very clear on what women need—someone to share their lives with and someone who makes them feel secure. I'm not quali-

fied to say that these are the only things women look for because I'm not one, but I can say those two things have been
important for every woman I've dealt with in any kind of way.
As hunters, we men understand this, and so we'll set out the
bait to meet those two needs, knowing that if we just give the
illusion of those two things, we get everything we want out of
you.

Of course, some relationships are built on this; the world is
full of women who want nothing more than to be sponsored—to
get a man's cash with no obligation to him. For every woman
like that, there are twenty men willing to sign up for the program because, just like she claims she doesn't want anything
more than money, he's clear that he doesn't want anything
more than the sex that comes with handing the money over.
If a man meets a woman who is physically to his liking and
she makes it perfectly clear she doesn't want anything but a
little financial help, then cool: we're used to that. We have to
pay for your company and sex anyway. So instead of taking
you to dinner and wining and dining you, let's package it all
up and call it rent. Instead of taking you on trips, let's add all
the money that would involve and call it a car note. And once
those things are paid for and the passionate moment has come
and gone, we're through. If you don't want anything emotionally, well hell, guess what? We don't want anything either.
Men are not dumb—they know when they're being gamed
for their cash. But trust me when I tell you: a man enters these
kinds of relationships willingly. You're not pulling the wool
over his eyes. And the moment he decides he's bored with you
or tired of the game, he'll simply move on—either to another

woman who has more excitement to offer, or to a woman whom he's decided to give his heart to. He's the master of the game. He knows what's up.

The moment you start expecting more from him is the moment you'll be in trouble. You may have liked being spoiled but as with any sugar high, eventually, you're going to crash; you're going to come down and crave something of substance. However, you won't get it. You'll have his cell-phone number but you won't be able to call him at the house; you'll be invited to his "house" but it won't look lived in (which means he probably has a real home with somebody somewhere else); you won't ever meet his family or go on double dates with his best friends (because no one else—especially his boy's girlfriend, who is likely friends with his real girlfriend—can see you, lest they give you and him a hard time); you won't ever sit next to him in a house of worship (even the hardest dogs of dogs won't push the limit with the Lord that far, and there aren't too many dudes who have that kind of dog in them). He's generous, but he's not sharing his life with you.

You will not get real companionship from him. You will not get him to protect, profess, or provide for you—to truly get him to show and prove his love for you. What's worse is that when Mr. Right does come along, you won't recognize him because your standards will be out of reach of what most well-intentioned men can provide; you'll miss the guy who is willing to pick you up on time and introduce you to his friends and sit in a house of worship with you on Sunday morning but doesn't have the money to, say, pay your rent. The man who is willing to give you true kindness, understanding, companionship, and attention doesn't have a chance because you've sold out for cash to pay your car note and rent.

Is the car note and rent worth that if what you ultimately want is a sound, secure, loving relationship?

So how do you get away from the sugar and find yourself some substance? Get back to what I told you in *Act Like a Lady, Think Like a Man*: get some standards and some requirements. A man can only act like a sugar daddy if you sign up for the program to be "sugared," I promise you. Trust me—I've seen it a million times. I've got plenty of friends who've played sugar daddy more times than they're willing to cop to. One of my boys had a fleet of gorgeous women he flew all around the country; he'd buy them things to keep them interested and have them coming and going as if he was running air traffic control at LAX. Arrival and departure times—that's all he cared about. I personally saw the doorman who controlled entry into his building high-five him one evening and say, "Sir, I'm enjoying your visits." He did nothing for those women—he didn't profess any love for them, he didn't take them to meet his family, there was no coming over to his house unannounced, and they weren't invited into his life to share it with him. He was just offering up sponsorship packages.

Then he met his match—a beautiful woman with her head on her shoulders who made clear to him that she wasn't about to sign up for the program. She made it very clear that she wasn't interested in how much he made or what he did for a living—she just wanted a man who would love her and be faithful. And she let him know, too, that she couldn't be bought—not with the typical things he used to get for the other women. Her purchase price was a mite higher: she told him how he was going to treat her, how he was going to deal with her, and how he was going to show his love to her. And he rose to the occasion. I swear to you, living with a woman like that is like living with corrections; whatever wrong mess you did before comes to a stop with her, and if you want to stay with her, you do what she wants you to do in order to keep her. She lets you know, too, that she's willing to walk away if you don't act right and quick.

That's the power you have in a true, valuable relationship. Convincing a man to give you things isn't power, I promise you that. When you sign up for a sugar daddy, all you're doing is delaying what is real—your true happiness—because a sugar daddy eventually goes away. The relationship is almost always temporary. Of course, some men are genuinely trying to help you, but plenty more are just playing and biding their time. The key to determining the difference is figuring out if you're getting what *you* need and really want. If you're taking the help but your relationship isn't going anywhere—he's not calling, he's consistently not showing up when he said he would, he's treating you like a throwback instead of a keeper (see the glossary)—then you're being used.

Now, I can't and I won't tell you not to accept gifts from a man; he might very well be the man of your dreams and he may want to give you something nice because that's what he wants to do for the woman with whom he can see himself. But please know he's giving you something because he wants something. Your job is to make clear what *you* want, and let him know that the true gift he can give—the one you're willing to accept with an open heart—is not material, it's true love. If he can't give that to you, then walk away.

Do you understand what I'm saying here? Walk. Away.

You've got to be willing to do this to get what you want. Don't be scared; if this man is giving you only the material things, but isn't being the kind of man you want, need, and deserve, leave him and open yourself up to someone better— the guy who is willing to do what it takes to keep you.

# PART II
# Finding a Man

# 5

~~➤~~——◆——◆

## THE STANDOFF

### He Won't Commit, You Won't Leave—Now What?

You've been dating for years. Your girlfriends, your sister, and even your worst enemy have been advising that it's about time he commit to you, but he's dragging his feet. Sound familiar? Know that you're not alone in trying to figure out why he just won't get on with it already. Single women across the land are talking about it on practically every television talk show, in nearly every women's magazine, and at many a girlfriend spa getaway session—men aren't committing. We are neither interested in nor care to be bothered with marriage. Plenty of statistics back this up, too: for example, a 2008 America's Families and Living Arrangements survey by the U.S. Bureau of the Census shows that the percentage of married men and women above age fifteen living in the United States hovers just around the 50 percent mark, which means that a significant number of women old enough to get hitched don't have a ring and about 46 percent of men old enough to wear a wedding ring aren't. Every year, too, the numbers of men and women heading to the altar to say "I do" takes a small dip—enough to sound the alarm on the prospects of finding a marriage partner.

Scary times if you want to be married.

Thing is, even as society keeps pushing on little girls, young ladies, and grown women the notion that they have to be married to be complete and secure, nobody is really preaching this to boys and men. Indeed, from practically the time we come out of the womb, we're told to play the field and take our time. And as we get older, we guard fiercely what we think are sane, rational reasons for staying single: it's easier to live with a woman than to be married to her; it's better to wait to have kids; we can get more sex if we're single; the woman we marry has to be absolutely perfect for us; it's cheaper to stay single than it is to pay alimony; and did I mention we can get more sex if we're single? We should be set in our careers and have money in our bank accounts before we think about taking on the responsibility of a wife and kids; we don't have to change or compromise if we stay single; and, oh yeah—we can get more sex if we're single.

With all those perfectly rational reasons and absolutely no pressure from anyone to get married, it's really no wonder that half of us old enough to get married don't. But this doesn't mean that we aren't *capable* of commitment. In fact, we commit to a lot of things: Tee times. Basketball games with our buddies. Our biweekly appointments at the barbershop. Our jobs. Our children. Our mortgages, leasing agreements, and car notes. Our friends.

And, yes, the women we love.

Men make those commitments when we are compelled to do so—when the consequences of not being committed are laid out and made clear to us. See, a man doesn't do anything unless he knows there's a sound reason for doing it. He commits to golf tee times because he knows that if he misses it, he may not get another until hours later, and his whole day will be thrown off. He commits to showing up on time to his weekend basketball game with the guys knowing that if he's late, he may not get to play until the second game. He commits to making his appointment at the barbershop knowing that if he doesn't show up at the right time, he might end up in the chair of the barber who is just learning his way around a pair of clippers. He commits to showing up to work on time knowing that if he's late, he loses pay; commits to paying his rent on time knowing that if he's late, he pays fines or loses his apartment; commits to paying his car note knowing that if he doesn't, his ride could get repossessed.

Men do all these things because troubling repercussions and consequences occur if they blow off those commitments. And the same is true of a man who knows he'll lose the woman he loves if he fails to fulfill his commitment to her. And let's be real here: though half the men of marrying age are not married, half of them are, and thousands more marriages occur every day. Why? Because many men are capable and do fulfill that commitment to their women. These men are not intimidated by their women (no matter how accomplished they are), they're not ashamed of their station in life, they're not dogs, they're not afraid of responsibility or of losing their freedom. They got married or are getting married because they love the women with whom they exchanged rings with, and, just as important, their women made marriage a requirement of their continuing the relationship.

Call me a hopeless romantic but I honestly believe your man is out there, and that getting into a solid, stable, loving relationship is still possible. Here's the rub: finding that commitment begins and ends with you. I know, I know. This places the responsibility squarely in your lap. But the reality is that women truly hold the power in their pretty, delicate, manicured hands. I said it in *Act Like a Lady, Think Like a Man*, but it bears repeating: a man can't hold a conversation with you, kiss you, hold your hand, call your house, take you out, or pull back the sheets on your bed except with your permission—period. You have the power, here, to decide if we're going to stop with all our foolishness or get away with it, and really, we can't make any meaningful moves without you. Think about it: a man can't run for president if he doesn't have a wife; other men aren't about to let some guy have all that power and have a nation of women—even their own—looking wistfully at a single president, and we all know full well that women bring all kinds of necessary nuances to the Oval Office. Look at recent events. A man who cheats on his wife and has a baby out of wedlock can't run for the presidency because his character is now in question; both women—his wife and his lover—hold the power to keep him from the most powerful seat in the land. That's power. A governor so whipped by the love of a woman clean on the other side of the world tells his staff, his wife, his children, and his state a pack of lies so he can get to the woman he loves—no matter the consequences. That's power. If we have children together, the law almost always allows you to keep them over us. Hell, we can't make those babies without you. That's power. Women help us curb our worst instincts; you're like our built-in moral compass, keeping us sane and out of a life of ridiculous, drunken debauchery. All too many of us would be out-of-control frat boys acting the fool all day, every day for the sum of the next thirty years; we'd spend every single cent we have on strippers and hookers, get drunk and stupid and do entirely inappropriate things every second of the day, if it weren't for our love and respect for our women, and your deep faith in us, keeping us in check. That's power.

Not only do we need you, we want you too.

But if you want more than one casual hookup after another with a man, you're going to have to show him the way to your heart and make him work to get there. You know the Bible verse: To whom much is given, much is required. This needs to be your motto—your modus operandi—as you seek a commitment from him; you have to let him know that you have a lot to offer and that you fully intend to use your powers for the good of the both of you, but only if he meets *your* requirements. Get commitment from your man by keeping the following in mind.

# HOW TO GET A MAN TO COMMIT

## 1. Get Yourself Ready for a Commitment

I'll never forget the lesson my mother taught me about getting ready for a blessing. I was living with my parents, trying to find my way, and preparing myself for big things—in this particular instance, a new car. My old car was sitting up on cinder blocks in my parents' driveway, and I'd been saving up my money and checking car dealerships and want ads all around town, looking for a more polished ride. One morning while we were enjoying breakfast together, I said, "Mama, I've been working really hard. I'm going to get a new car," seeking out support.

At first, she didn't say anything—just nodded. And then she reminded me: "Your old car is out there on the blocks."

A couple days later, I announced to her my intentions again, and again, she nodded and repeated what seemed obvious: "Your old car is out there on the blocks."

For the life of me, I couldn't understand why my mother, who was usually much more supportive, appeared only lukewarm about my plans for a new car. The only enthusiasm she could muster up whenever the subject came up was that "your old car is out there on the blocks" statement. And by the fourth time she said it to me, I confronted her. "Mama, how come every time I say I want a new car, you tell me about my old one?"

She was quiet at first. And then she let me have it: "If God gives you a new car, where are you going to put it? Your old car is out there on the blocks. If you're going to ask God for something, act like he's going to give it to you and make ready to receive it."

And you know what? What she said made all the sense in the world. I wasn't ready for a new car because my old one was taking up space out there in the driveway. Like trash. Even if Ed McMahon had driven up in a new car, I wouldn't have had a space for it until I cleaned up my mess. That's just what I did, too. I called one of my partners and paid him twenty-five dollars to tow that car away. Then I hosed off the concrete and put down some new asphalt and cleared out those blocks and got that driveway ready for my new ride. Two months later, I drove my new car onto that nice, clean driveway and thanked God for my blessing. Finally, I was ready to receive it.

I share this metaphor with you because it symbolizes what women who truly are looking for a committed relationship must do to get ready for the blessing. You can't get the man you want if you got all your garbage—all that baggage from the last guy who did you wrong, an ex you won't let go of—in your figurative driveway, up on those blocks. You simply have no room in your heart if the guy you keep dating, even though you know he's not the one for you, is hanging around. You may touch each other every once in a while and do things to make each other feel good, but on balance you're lonely, he's not there for you when you need him, and you know that relationship isn't going anywhere. He's like that old car up there on those blocks, taking up space.

The same is true of things that block your heart and your

mind from being available for someone new—divorce, bitterness over a relationship gone wrong, holding on to the myth that all the good guys are taken, thinking it's best to have a deep bench of guys to "play" with rather than focusing on making one relationship work. Each of these things keeps your heart up on those blocks—makes you seek out in the new guy all the mistakes and screwups that ended the last relationship, hold on to the bitterness, and brace yourself for something bad when you should be focused on finding something good.

You've got to stop looking for all the signs that the new man is going to hurt you, stop messing around with the guy who's just wasting your time, stop holding on to the hurt and anger and resentment that came from your divorce. Call the tow truck and haul that mess out of there, and get ready to receive the man who is worthy of you.

## 2. Build a Fence Around Your Heart

To do this, you're first going to have to let go of the stereotypes that paint men with that broad stroke of negativity. Contrary to popular belief and a host of bad information passed down from generation to generation of girlfriends, there are some good men out there. You wouldn't know it by the stories many women share with one another: all the good men are taken. Men don't want to commit, they just want to play. They just want to have sex with as many women as possible and don't care about your feelings. If you hear this enough, you internalize it, then transfer the stereotypes to every man standing before you—whether he fits the mold or is the very antithesis of it. Once that image is etched on your mind, then you're setting the tone for how you're going to present yourself to the men who do come your way. You know how it works: He could meet you one glorious Saturday afternoon in the park—the sun could be shining, the birds could be chirping, and he could be as charming, funny, intelligent, and handsome as you'd have him to be, but in the back of your mind, the loop of conversations between you and your girlfriend plays on and on. The moment he answers a question the wrong way, you're making assumptions about him and changing the way you're presenting yourself to him. All of a sudden where there was a smile, there is attitude. Where there was spirit, there is defeat. Where there was hope, there is brooding. All because he said he doesn't want to get married right away or doesn't want kids right now. He may have meant, "I don't want to get married before I finish school," but because you've bought into the stereotypes about men and commitment, you hear, "I don't want to be married ever."

In essence, you build a twenty-foot brick wall with barbed wire at the top. I promise you, few men are going to be willing to scale it. Your presentation, your approach, your energy isn't welcoming—nothing about you is saying to prospective suitors, "I'm available, approachable, and, under the right conditions, ready for love." Sure you could be screaming it from the tower window through a megaphone a mile away from the fence you built, but he's not going to hear you because you're too far away, too high up, and too guarded.

Don't get me wrong: there's nothing wrong with standards.

In fact, I've always said that you have the right to have them—*must* have them in order to get a man to take a relationship with you seriously. But do your standards and requirements reflect who you are and what you're capable of giving back? Because not many men will sign up for a situation that isn't fairly equal. I remember when I presented *Act Like a Lady, Think Like a Man* on *Oprah*, there was a woman in the audience who said she had a list with two hundred thirty-six standards and requirements, and any man who wanted to be with her had to meet every last one of them. One of them I distinctly remember was that she wanted a man who is at least six feet, four inches, with a nice build and washboard abs, and that she had no intentions of settling for less. Well, I remember sitting there looking and thinking to myself, "If I were six feet, four inches with washboard abs, I'm not about to pick soft, short, and fluffy. I'm in the gym working my ass off, eating turnip greens and tofu, and you're chowing down on smothered pork chops? No ma'am."

You can have all the high standards you want and demand a man scale that twenty-foot barbwire fence just to go on a date or two with you. But the last thing you want him to say when he makes it over there is, "Damn: You made me climb over all of this and this is all you got?!" Why does he have to be a millionaire if you're working at the shoe store? Why demand he have three degrees when, despite your native intelligence, you dropped out of junior college? Why demand he own and run a business if you can't even pull together bus fare to make it to your job? Why expect him to treat you with respect, and be kind and loving and sweet, if on every personality test you take, words like *bossy*, *full of attitude*, and *aggressive* come up. This is what folks mean when they suggest your standards might be too high. You may have met him because you had on a miniskirt and some pumps and had a glowing tan, but he's not going to stop and notice, much less scale, that tall wall of yours if you're not giving him a reason to.

That doesn't mean you lower or eliminate your standards and requirements altogether, either. You don't build a one-foot fence around your yard and then let just any old body walk all over your lawn. If you have no standards and requirements, a man can cancel a date with you at the last minute without repercussion, he can sleep with you before you've got ninety days' (more of that in the glossary) worth of dating under your belt, and he can call you two hours after he told you he would and then show up in the middle of the night for the infamous booty call. You're essentially signing up to be mistreated by someone for whom commitment doesn't matter. And trust me: if a man thinks he can have you without making a commitment, you're not going to get a commitment from him.

If you truly want commitment, you're going to have to build a four-foot fence around your heart—raise your standards up in a way that says, "Not everybody can come and play and dance in my yard. If you want to act disrespectfully, then go up the street to someone else's yard." It is those standards and requirements—the demanding he treat you with respect, the requiring him to call when he says he's going to call and take you out when he says he's going to take you out, his rising to the occasion and being good with your kids, and, most important, his acknowledging that you require commitment from any man coming into your yard—that will make him under-

stand that to get past that fence, he's got to put in some work.
But the work will be well worth it because behind that fence is
a beautiful prize: your love, your support, and your cookie
(more on that in Chapter 8 and the glossary)—the three things
every man needs to feel whole with a woman.

## RECOGNIZE WHY YOU'RE STICKING AROUND

A woman is programmed from the time she sees her first Disney
movie to expect that a knight in shining armor will ride in on
his big white horse and whisk her off to their big wedding day,
with all the doves chirping, the flowers blooming, and the
townspeople cheering her on as she rides off into the sunset
with Prince Charming—right on into her happily ever after.
This is part of the female culture and you start getting messages
even as a toddler: you should expect to get married, have a
family, and grow old with someone you love who loves you
back. There's nothing wrong with wanting that dream; it
doesn't have to be a fairy tale. But if your pursuit of that dream
wedding is keeping you in a relationship that offers no hope of
commitment, no chance of advancement, and is doing nothing
more than making you miserable, then your dream of happily
ever after will never become reality. And though you may not
want to hear or accept it, you really have no one else to blame
for this but yourself.

This is harsh, I know, but it's the truth.

You're stuck in a relationship with a man who isn't fully

committing to you because you're not using your power to make him understand that you will accept nothing less than commitment. Please understand: a man who wants you will jump through hoops of fire with buckets of gasoline tied to his waist if he loves you and you make clear to him that you need a firm commitment from him—monogamy and a ring—if he's going to stay with you. We understand consequences; it's what we live and die by. But if you're letting him stick around, without demanding he make his intentions clear, and you're conducting your relationship under the premise that "some" man is better than "no" man, then you're going to get what you signed up for: just a piece of a man.

Men understand why you stay. You rationalize it's better to keep us and be halfway happy, even if you don't get your wedding day and the paper that says you're officially committed to each other, than to risk being alone. But you've got to take a less emotional approach and think logically about why staying with him, if you're doing it for any of the following four reasons, isn't in your best interest.

## 1. If You're Staying with Him Because of the Kids

I commend you for this—it's a noble gesture. No child should have to grow up without a father in the home, and it's a natural part of your nurturing instinct to want your kids to stay in an intact household if it's an option. There's value to that. But what value does your child get when he sees his mother is miserable all the time? Who wins if you're doing all the cooking, all the cleaning, all the child rearing, making all the effort and getting back more than your share of misery or frustration, and you're not getting what you want and need in return? Is it win-win if your child doesn't know what love and respect look like? I've even heard women say that for the sake of their children, they're simply going to stick it out in their relationship arrangements until their kids graduate from school, and then they'll leave. That's a mighty long time to wait for happiness. That's why they have this thing called visitation. You should look into that. And then make plans to get happy, particularly if he's the type who's never going to give you the commitment you need.

## 2. If You're Staying with Him Hoping That He'll Eventually Give You a Ring

Know that the ring's not coming. You've been with him for how long and he still hasn't asked you? He's still making excuses and promises? He never wants to talk about taking the next step? Tells you he's not ready? Those are all the signs that you're holding on to a hope that's absolutely hopeless. He's not marrying you because you're not telling him it's mandatory in order for the two of you to continue. Why should he? He says he loves you. You've had his children and he's grateful for his babies. You're sleeping with him. You hold him when he's sad. His family already accepts you. And you're going to the office parties. He's got all of the benefits of a marriage. In his mind there's no compelling reason to get married. You're the one who wants a wedding. He doesn't and until you make it a requirement, he won't.

## 3. If You're Staying Because the Sex Is Good

Fireworks at night will leave you feeling nothing but empty and alone in the morning. Countless women will tell you in a heartbeat, "I can't bear him—he's not doing this, he's not doing that, but girl, all the lights swirl and the stars pop in the sky when I'm in bed with him!" His physical prowess is so outstanding, that moment of gratification is so addictive, all his negatives are overlooked for a moment of sexually charged excitement. But let me clue you in on a little something: he's not the only one who can satisfy you. If you really want to experience something incredible, find a man who treats you the way you deserve to be treated, a man who adores you the way you deserve to be adored and gives you your heart's desires. See how that feels. Talk about "Oh say can you see" and bombs bursting in the air! You're diminishing your chances of getting true gratification as long as you keep messing around with the wrong one.

## 4. If You're Staying Because the Money Is Right

Know that you're selling your happiness to the highest bidder. Let's say he's the primary breadwinner—he makes more than you or his half is essential to upholding the lifestyle you're accustomed to and have come to love. You're going to take a hit if you leave; you may go from a mansion to an apartment, from a luxury car to a used sedan, from expendable income to a scenario where you're closer to living paycheck to paycheck. But isn't that worth your happiness? Can you put a price tag on what your happiness is worth? What's the cost? Is it worth $36,000 a year? $100,000? $1 million? Are the big house, the two extra cars, and the shopping sprees at the fancy stores worth the misery? You may lose financially if you walk away, but what you gain in happiness, peace of mind, and self-esteem—is priceless.

## BE WILLING TO CASH IN YOUR CHIPS

Once you consider all of the preceding, once you think logically about how illogical it is to hold on to a man who refuses to give you what you want, you're going to have to take that brave step and stop gambling with your life. Because that's all you're doing. You're going from table to table, winning some and losing some, collecting chips before giving them up. This ain't Vegas, baby. What happens here stays with you for the rest of your life. Getting married is more than just the pretty wedding gown and the flavor of cake you'll serve, deciding who'll be in the wedding party and the size of the stone in the ring; a lot of rights come with that piece of paper that says you are legally bound to this man. If something happens to the husband, the job and Social Security will pay benefits to his wife and the children. If he gets sick and medical decisions need to be made at the hospital, a girlfriend doesn't have any decision-making power (common law exceptions notwithstanding), no matter how long she's been with her man, no matter how often they talked about what his wishes would be were he ever in the position where life-and-death decisions had to be made. A wife has that power. If a man decides to break up with a woman who's been in a long-term relationship with him and helped him build his wealth, the ex-girlfriend has no claim on the money they accumulated together, but if she's got marriage papers, she gets half.

Why would you gamble with your life like that? Something could happen next month, and you'd have nothing to show for all of the work you put in. Trust me: he's got plenty—he's got you, he's got sex, he's got emotional support, he's got your loyalty, and he's still got his freedom to leave whenever he wants with very few repercussions. Shouldn't you have what you want too? If you want him to commit, he has to know that you will cash the chips in—that you will leave. Otherwise, again, most men will not voluntarily head to the altar. You can tell your children all day, "If you don't do this, that, and the other, you're going to be in big trouble," but until you show them what will happen to them if they don't listen, they will keep testing you. Hate to compare men to children but let's keep it real.

Don't let men do that to you; take your chips up to the window and cash them in. Let him know that the consequence of not giving you what you want is he'll be left alone—without you. Men absolutely will not do anything without a reason, and the reason we do most things is so that we can get the attention of the opposite sex. It's a core tenet of manhood. We go to school because we know that if we go to college, there will be girls there. We go to college and get a degree so we can get a good-paying job so we can flash our money around to attract women. We want to be the star in the football game and say we're the quarterback because young women will love the letter jacket. Little boys run faster, climb higher, and jump longer when they know a girl is watching. They will knock themselves out if a girl is looking, honest to goodness. My family and I went on vacation recently and my son Wynton was at the beach with his sister Lori. When two Brazilian girls hopped in the water, he started doing underwater headstands. I had to run and go get my son because he was damn near drowning himself—choking and coughing and clawing at his face after salt got into his eyes—all because he was showing off for these girls. A few weeks later, he almost knocked me out when he came running down the stairs wearing an entire can of TAG body spray after he saw a commercial showing ten girls jumping all over this guy who was wearing it. He did those crazy things for a reason: because he wanted to capture the attention and heart of the opposite sex.

This doesn't change when men get older: we do things to impress you, and we listen to and abide by your rules and requirements if the consequences of not doing so mean we're going to lose you. My buddy's grandmother once said to me that the finest woman in the world is your ex on the arm of another man. And, buddy, let me tell you what we can't stand to see: the woman we've been intimate with, lived with, built a future with, dreamed about a better day with, on the arm of another man. We can't take that.

Sure, there's a chance that when you make that ultimatum—when you demand that commitment—he'll move on. Let. Him. Go. If he was willing to walk away from what you had to offer, he was a noncontender anyway. Sure, you invested time in this guy, sure you love him, sure you want to be with him. But you also want what you want, and you have the right to want that commitment from him—you have the right to stand firm on this.

Just like men don't change, women don't either—and that's okay. If you want it at twenty-five, you're going to want it at thirty-five. What's not so okay is compromising your requirements to justify having a relationship with a man who won't give you what you ultimately want; settling is compromising. What's not okay is burying your want and need for security, protection, respect, and support. Yielding and bending to his will—pushing aside what you want—is compromising. And when you compromise who you are for a man, there's no way you can find a deep, long-lasting happiness. If you're not happy, you're not loving him the way he needs to be loved—you're not supporting him, you're not loyal to him, and you're less willing to give him the cookie. And if he's not getting those three things, the relationship gets more dysfunctional and less pleasant until one of you finally leaves.

I'm not asking you to change for him. I'm telling you to understand his thought process, set your requirements, and stand firm on them so that you can get what *you* want: commitment. And if he can't give that to you—if he refuses—cut your losses. Push those chips up to the window and tell him you're not gambling with your life anymore.

He may move on. But if he has searched his heart and loves you, he'll stay.

Either way, long term, you win.

The bottom line is that the world is full of men who are willing and able to commit. Get your house in order, put your standards and requirements to use, exercise your power in your relationships, and be willing to walk away. I'm not saying this journey will be easy or quick. But it'll be well worth it.

# TWELVE WAYS TO TELL IF YOUR MAN IS READY TO COMMIT

1. He takes you to his place of worship.
2. He thinks about you when you're away and still thinks about you when you're near.
3. He changes all his phone numbers so that none of his old flames can contact him anymore.
4. He allows you to help pick out his wardrobe.
5. Any man who wears matching outfits is totally committed because he has lost *all* his friends' respect.
6. He gives you a nickname he can't allow his friends to hear, like Schmoogles. Trust me, he knows full well that as soon as his friends hear that, they'll know he's sprung and, though it's your nickname, that's what they'll call *him* every time they see him.
7. He puts making you happy in front of his own happiness.
8. He's seen you without your hair styled and no makeup and still keeps calling.
9. He's met your entire family and is still willing to attend the family reunion.
10. He knows your kids are crazy and ill-mannered but loves you anyway.
11. He's seen your mother in action and still thinks you can make it as a couple.
12. He allows you to meet *his* entire family, realizing this could change everything.

For Ladies Only . . .

## SOMETIMES, THE BREAKUP IS A BLESSING

I know it's hard when you leave someone you've loved; it's painful, emotional, and leaves a mark on your heart that feels like an open wound. But there's a blessing in the storm, I promise you. You just have to recognize it and claim it for yourself. All too often, women stay in relationships because they've got some serious time invested, even though there is constant fighting, you've got very little in common, and you've grown in different directions. I know people who are married who don't even like each other, but still, they hang on. I ask, what are you hanging on to? Know that if you just let go, the chances are that you'll wake up in peace. The arguing will be gone. So will the fighting. You'll get to do what you want to do without having to cater to a man who doesn't appreciate what you're doing. First, though, you have to remember what you're breaking up from: if you've been cheated on, lied to, abused, left to spend all your time alone, forced to constantly question his whereabouts, then you're not leaving much. Let go of it and claim your blessing. You may be hurt, alone, and scared of getting back into the dating game, but this is the alone time you need to better position yourself for what the Creator has in mind for you. What He has in mind for you may be just waiting for you to be free and available. The blessing is that you can reinvent yourself—be who you want to be instead of who you had to be in order to make that past relationship work. I can truly attest to the blessings that come when you become open to change. If I had focused on trying to get into acting, I can assure you I wouldn't have the success I have today. If I just did stand-up, I would have never gotten the *Steve Harvey Show*. If I stayed on the show, I would have never gotten on the radio. If I had focused on radio, I never would have written the book. If I'd never written the book, I never would have gotten the international acclaim that comes from my book-buying audience. I'm constantly reinventing myself, and you shouldn't be afraid to reinvent yourself. If you're getting out of a toxic relationship, the blessing is that he can't throw you down the steps anymore; if you're getting out of a relationship in which your man was unfaithful, the blessing is that you don't have to sit and wonder and worry about who he's with at night. If you're getting out of a relationship in which your kids saw you arguing and fighting and mad all the time, the blessing is that the kids don't have to witness you feeling sad and depressed anymore— they can see you happy again. Look at the positives and "do you." Get back to the hobbies you liked doing before you got with him. Go out with your girls like you used to before your relationship took precedence. Spend some time getting really clear about what, exactly, it is you want for yourself before you get into another relationship. And when the new you emerges, you'll be a better you. And the better you attracts what? A better man. And both of these are a blessing.

# 6

## LET'S STOP THE GAMES

### Asking Men the *Right* Questions
### to Get the *Real* Answers

I admit it—simple as we men claim to be, we can be tricky creatures, especially when it comes to women. We are the masters of the okey-doke and will dole out affection in drips and drops and use them as emotional placeholders until we decide in our own minds whether we really want to be with you or we want to move on to the next conquest. We'll send the sweet text message to get you swooning, but then go for days without calling. We'll spend the whole of a month wining and dining you and making you feel like there's some amazing chemistry between us, but then clam up when it comes time to explain what, exactly, our intentions are concerning the relationship. We do this because we can. We can because all too many women let us. All too many women let us because they're afraid of the alternative—having to start all over again with a new man, or having no man at all.

I wrote both in *Act Like a Lady, Think Like a Man* and in Chapter 5 ("The Standoff") of this book that women truly interested in finding the right guy have to get over the fear of losing one, because the moment you lose that fear is the moment guys lose their power over you. A man will disrespect you, put in minimal effort, and hold out on commitment if he thinks he can get away with it, so your job is to not let him get away with it. But this requires heading off the foolishness at the beginning—before a man gets his hooks in you—so that you can make clear-eyed decisions, devoid of emotion, about whether to continue pursuing a relationship with him. So much can be found out about a guy before you get in too deep—if you take the time to ask the right questions. I'm not referring here to the five general questions every woman should ask a man when she's getting to know him (see the glossary), though asking those questions, as explained in the first book, will help you figure out what a potential mate wants out of life and what he wants out of a relationship with you; learning how to probe his answers will help you get to the very essence of who this man is and whether he has what you're looking for in a long-lasting relationship.

To do this successfully, though, you'll have to wrap your head around and understand one basic thing about us men: no matter the question, we will always give you the answer that will make us look the best.

Plain and simple.

I'm willing to wager that in the history of your relationships, you've never had a man introduce himself and share with you all his baggage and all his bad habits in the first several dates. You're an adult; you know full well everyone comes with a history—everyone comes with a backstory and flaws. Yet if every man's story was as good as the story he reveals about himself, you would have found your Prince Charming by now. Why aren't you with the *perfect* man? Why? Because no one is that good.

Knowing that you long to be needed and wanted, however, men prey on those vulnerabilities; we manipulate our answers and the impressions we make so that we appear to be the man who can fulfill all those needs and wants—we sell the Happily Ever After. Tell a guy you're looking for a man who is capable of commitment, and if he's truly interested in you, he'll have no problem telling you he wants exclusivity too. What he's not going to offer up is that his last relationship didn't work out because he cheated. Tell a man you'd like to be in a relationship with a guy who is good with kids, and he's going to regale you with proud stories about how much he loves his nieces and nephews. But he's probably going to keep to himself the information about his wicked baby mama drama, or the fact that he doesn't see his kids but once every other month. And I promise you, you're not going to hear on your first date about a man's bad credit, his house foreclosure, or that he lived with his mother until five weeks ago; instead, this guy is going to go out of his way to show you his nice watch, his slick suit, and the nice car he barely held on to during his own personal economic crisis.

Men do this because we think that if we release this information too early, we won't get the catch—you. You have to remember that at the base of it, we're no different from, say, a peacock with a plume of colorful feathers, or a lion with a huge, bushy, fiery orange mane: just like a male peacock spreading those feathers or a male lion standing tall among his pride to attract their female counterparts, men flash things like their money, their cars, their clothes, their watches, and their job titles to impress women. The presentation is critical to us—it's all part of the bait we throw in the water to capture the fish; we just want you to bite on the hook. A man knows he's not hooking any woman with stories about how broke he is or how he doesn't have any power at his job or how his ex-wife comes around the house every Thursday to scrawl "He's completely unreliable" in red chalk across the garage doors. He's wrapping himself in all the pretty packaging so you'll buy into him.

Come on, admit it: women tend to ask men two questions, tops, before they make the decision about whether a man might just be the one for them. Knowing this, we'll answer the first question in a way that'll make us come out smelling like a rose. Ask a follow-up question for a little clarification, and we'll find an even slicker way to tell you what you want to hear. And once a man tells you what makes him sound the best, you hear what you want to hear and, instead of asking more questions and getting to the truth of the matter, you form your own truth. You get so enamored by his buzzwords—I want to be committed, I love kids, I'm a hard worker, I love to cook, I'm into the arts—that you skip asking more questions and immediately start saying to yourself, "It's him! It's him! Oh, thank you Lord, I found him!" You take the good parts—the answers to the first two levels of questioning—bundle up those words and internalize them, then use them to justify falling in love with who you think is the "ideal" man, never considering—often, until it's too late—that had you probed a little deeper you would have gotten closer to who he really is.

You don't dig deeper because you're scared that if the questions run too deep, he will run off and you will lose out on a good one. He doesn't tell the whole truth because he's scared he might not appeal to you. Everybody is just scared now. Scared and avoiding the *whole* truth.

Don't buy into the fairy tale. Sure, men would serve themselves well if they provided the relevant information up front; not only would it clear men from ever being accused of lying—a charge that adds a lot more tollbooths on the road to solid relationships—but certainly it would give the women we truly want to build relationships with more insight into who we really are. All too often, we men prevent the relationship from growing because we create an element of distrust early on, by withholding vital information that gives women that which they need to make sound decisions for themselves. When a woman gets blindsided with information she thinks should have been disclosed up front, she questions everything—no matter a man's intentions.

So should men offer all the information up front? Of course we should. It's only fair. But we won't volunteer it because telling the whole truth not only makes us look lesser in your eyes, but it also takes the "chase and capture" out of our hands and puts the future of the relationship squarely into yours. A man's candidness early on gives you the chance to truly understand how, for example, past relationships might affect your future together; the opportunity to process the information; and the ability to decide for yourself if you can handle the baggage that comes with all the good he's already told you about. Sure, there are some men who will lay out all the dirty laundry up front for you to see. But this is rare. Very rare. So the onus of getting down to the truth is, unfortunately, on you.

And you get to the truth by digging deeper.

Aren't you tired of being the victim? Tired of getting played? Tired of thinking you got somebody and then finding out he's not all he made himself out to be? Stop giving up the cookie before you have all the information, and instead get the information and then decide if it's in your best interest to share yourself with him.

Doing this will take no more than three questions, I promise you. It hardly ever changes with us:

**Question No. 1** will get you the answer that makes us look best.

**Question No. 2** will get you the answer that we think you want to hear.

**Question No. 3** will introduce you to the truth.

We have no other choice but to tell the truth after that; our liar bench isn't deep enough to go up against your intuition, especially when you start probing us in that slick way only women can pull off. Witness:

## QUESTION NO. 1:
## WHY DID YOUR LAST RELATIONSHIP BREAK UP?

*The Answer That Makes Him Look Best:*

Well, I was trying to be all I could be—I was working hard, trying to provide for her, and she didn't understand my work ethic and she just couldn't take it anymore.

*The Breakdown:*

This answer makes him seem like he's a hard worker, committed to building toward the future. It also plays into a woman's natural instincts to be nurturing—makes you say to yourself, "I would never leave a man who's trying his best— I'd focus on supporting him."

## QUESTION NO. 2:
## IF SHE WERE MORE SUPPORTIVE, WOULD YOU HAVE STAYED IN THE RELATIONSHIP?

*The Answer That You Want to Hear:*

Absolutely. I want to be committed. I want to be with somebody who understands me and wants to be with me and understands what I'm about. I'm looking for that type of woman who wants to be committed and supportive of her man.

*The Breakdown:*

He's telling you what you want to hear—that he's a man who is committed and looking for a long-term relationship and willing to do what is necessary to take care of you. He knows those are all the buzzwords that get you hooked, and now he'll sit back and let you fill in all the blanks—imagine him walking out of the house in the morning, briefcase in hand, going to work hard for you and the family, then coming home and holding and caressing you in his strong arms until you fall asleep. Of course, he didn't say any of that other stuff; he just said what you wanted to hear. Don't fall for the okey-doke. Get to the bottom of it with this. . .

## QUESTION NO. 3:

## WELL, IF YOU WERE SUPPORTIVE, YOU WERE LOOKING FOR LOYALTY, AND YOU'RE A HARD WORKER AND A GOOD PROVIDER, HOW COULD THE RELATIONSHIP BREAK UP? WHAT HAPPENED THAT SHE SAID, "I CAN'T DO THIS ANYMORE"?

*The Truth:*

Well, I was looking for that support because I couldn't find it at home, and I met someone who was more supportive and loyal.

*The Breakdown:*

The only thing left for him to do was to admit that it was infidelity, rather than a nonsupportive woman, that led to his breakup. Of course, there are nuances to why he ended up cheating, but the fact is that the relationship ultimately ended because he was being unfaithful—he broke the cardinal rule. Now you know he's a hardworking guy who requires support and loyalty to be in a relationship, but you also know that he's capable of cheating if he feels like he's not getting what he needs out of the relationship.

*H*ere's another example.

I coached a listener on my radio show, the *Steve Harvey Morning Show*, to dig deeper into her questions with her man when she wrote that she suspected he wasn't quite the father he made himself out to be. "He says he's a great father," she wrote, "and speaks highly of both his son and his daughter . . ."

## QUESTION NO.1:
## HOW'S YOUR RELATIONSHIP WITH YOUR CHILDREN?

*The Answer That Makes Him Look Best:*

It's great. When we're together, it's nothing short of magical. My son is just like me—athletic and strong. And my daughter is smart and so beautiful. They're amazing kids.

*The Breakdown:*

This answer makes him seem like he's a fantastic dad, committed to his children and putting in work to mold them into good human beings. It plays into your natural desire for a man who will faithfully and happily participate in the rearing of the family you hope to have someday.

## QUESTION NO. 2:
## HOW IS YOUR RELATIONSHIP WITH THEIR MOTHER?

*The Answer That You Want to Hear:*

It's cool. We do what we can to get along for the sake of the kids. She doesn't make it easy, but my kids are worth it.

*The Breakdown:*

He's telling you what you want to hear—painting a picture of himself as the good guy in a relationship gone bad and the man who is willing to endure suffering and strife if it means he'll get to be with his kids. Now, he's looking like a super-hero in your eyes because there is nothing sexier to a woman than a man who will bend steel and leap tall buildings to get to his children. You start imagining him rubbing your pregnant belly and reading to your babies and standing over the grill cooking up a home-cooked meal for the entire family while you stand by, looking on admirably at your magnificent catch of a man. What you missed was that he said his ex doesn't make it easy for him to see his kids, and that he sees them when he can, not necessarily on a regular basis, and certainly not in the most pleasant of circumstances. Get to the bottom of it with this . . .

## QUESTION NO. 3:

## IF YOU AND THEIR MOTHER DON'T REALLY GET ALONG, HOW DOES THAT HINDER YOUR RELATIONSHIP WITH YOUR KIDS?

*The Truth:*

Well, because she and I don't really get along, it's hard for me to see them as much. I see them maybe once a month and talk to them occasionally on the phone. But there's some distance there because of the drama with my ex.

*The Breakdown:*

The only thing left for him to do was to admit that he's got some baby mama drama that keeps him from being the super-daddy he originally made himself out to be. The mother of his children may have good reason for cutting back on his time with his kids, or she could be a lunatic; in either case, you'd have some issues to deal with if you got into a relationship with this man—namely a potentially dramatic and volatile relationship with his ex, and some real inadequacies he may have as a father.

Getting to the bottom of that information allows you to make an informed decision about whether you want to start something with this guy. It's not hard—women are inquisitive by nature. You and your girlfriends ask these same questions when you recount your dates for each other anyway. You and your girls get to the bottom of things quickly. Do the same with him. Put aside all the romantic notions and approach this thing with eyes wide open and a clear mind.

My wife, Marjorie, played this really well when we started dating again. Of course, she was already privy to my shenanigans; I'm a public figure so there was already a lot of bad stuff about me out there—all she had to do was a simple Google search and everything she ever wanted to know about me, the good, the bad, the ugly, and the lies, was right there at her fingertips. I came in the door with publicized relationships gone bad. My advantage was that Marjorie already knew the real me; we'd been friends for twenty years and dated a few times by the time we got back together, so she knew there was some good there. A lot of good. But to figure out if I was truly ready to share that good with her, Marjorie knew I was going to have to add up some things for her. First, she asked why my first two marriages didn't work. I had a pat explanation at the ready:

"I was on the road touring and it kept me away from home a lot," I said simply. "The separation just grew and kept us apart and I wasn't there enough. I was working and trying to make it for us, but bringing home a check wasn't enough."

My veiled attempt to end this line of questioning by telling Marjorie I was committed and hardworking was no match for her; she kept the questions coming. "But what specifically made you decide those marriages weren't for you? Is it that marriage isn't for you?"

I brought my A-game on that one—told her what I thought she wanted to hear. "Well, I'm a romantic and I love the idea of being married. I want a committed relationship, I want a family, and that hasn't changed just because the first two marriages didn't work out. I have a lot, but I really want someone to share it with—a woman who can be loyal to me, who will support me while I'm out doing what I have to do to take care of our family, a woman who wants to share all the blessings in my life." I gave her details about how it all went down—about how my first marriage ended after I went away to become a comedian, and some of the problems that grew from my second marriage too.

Now, I thought I'd made it through—that I'd said what it took to get Marjorie hooked on the idea of being with me. But she just wouldn't let it go; she needed more from me—not because she was trying to give me a hard time, but because she really needed to make sure that her heart was protected. See, she'd already been through two marriages that didn't work, and she was in a good place—raising her kids, working hard, and really secure in knowing what she needed out of her next relationship. She'd made very clear that she didn't need to be in a relationship to be happy—that being alone was okay. But if she was going to get into another relationship, she needed to make sure that not only was she ready for it, but that any future mate was ready too. So a few days after our initial discussions, Marjorie pitched the third question: "I get that when you started telling jokes things weren't the same, but why did you just go away? Help me understand this thing."

I'd already told her what made me look best (I'm a hard worker), and in the second conversation, I told her what I thought she wanted to hear (I'm a romantic looking for a partner with which to share this journey). But in response to this third question? There wasn't any more carpet and cushioning I could put on the floors, no curtains I could use to dress up the windows, no faux finishes I could throw up on the walls to make me look better. I'd run out of ways to decorate the truth, and it was clear to me that she wasn't going to stop with the questions until she got the truth, so the truth was what I had to give her. And when I opened up to her, I revealed to Marjorie that the truth was that I was too young to get married the first time—that I should never have been anybody's husband at twenty-four. I didn't have it together in any way and really, the shortcomings in our relationship were mine—I was to blame, not my ex. All I could do in that first marriage was protect my wife and profess my love for her, but I simply wasn't capable of *providing* for her in any meaningful way. Not only couldn't I provide, I didn't even have a plan for providing. I knew from age nine that I wanted to be on television, but I wasn't doing anything useful to make that happen; I'd gone to college and gotten kicked out, and while I was working at the Ford Motor Company, I dreamed about being a star but had no real, tangible way of becoming one. "If my ex didn't believe in my future, I couldn't say I even saw it for myself," I told Marjorie. "Still, I resented her and anyone else who didn't support my vision. So really, I couldn't stick around for that."

I went on to tell her about how by the time I got married the second time, my career was in bloom and that I started enjoying the fruits of my labor in ways that were destructive to my relationship. Regardless of the reasons why I did that, when I was forced to really dig deep into what went awry, I always came to the same conclusion: my actions were wrong; I wasn't conducting myself in a way that was conducive to a successful marriage.

By probing, Marjorie really got to the truth with me. Admitting that I was resentful, didn't have a plan, and walked out on my first wife because I didn't have *my* act together didn't make me look like a good guy, by any stretch. Admitting to cheating on my second definitely wasn't going to make my case any easier. But it was the truth, and that truth gave Marjorie the chance to really come to terms with what she was signing up for, and, honestly, made me dig deeper into how my own personal shortcomings needed to be checked if I was going to make a marriage with Marjorie work.

After that conversation, Marjorie looked at me more closely and watched my actions and acknowledged that I was different now—that I was doing what it took to make our relationship work. When I was on the road, I would send for her every chance I could, she knew she could call the apartment anytime and I'd answer the phone, and if she was with me, I wasn't sleeping with my cell phone duct taped to my thigh so that she couldn't keep an eye on who was calling and texting me. She saw a man who was shedding the baggage and ready for real love, and she liked what she saw. And it wasn't long before she was saying, "I want you. You're the man for me."

But she had to come to that on her own, after gathering her information, evaluating it, and coming to some conclusions about what she would and would not tolerate. She didn't go about it in any nasty, mean way; she simply asked the right questions and kept digging until she got to the treasure—the truth.

Know that you can do this, too, and that you're going to have to be just as smooth and persistent about it. You can't grill this guy like you're Bill Duke in that scene from *Menace II*

*Society*, where the main character is sitting under the bright light in the interrogation room, sweating and stuttering while Bill stares at him with those piercing eyes and announces, "You know you effed up, don't you?" every time his suspect opened his mouth. No guy is going to willingly stick around for the lie detector test and the military-styled interrogation tactics.

What we will do, though, is answer truthfully over a period of time. Asking those questions during the ninety-day period I told you about in *Act Like a Lady, Think Like a Man* will give you plenty of time to learn the truth. If you really want to get to the bottom of it all, tell a guy, "I'm just looking for honesty—it really turns me on when a man tells the truth," and he's going to pull out all the stops because the mere promise of an eventual romp in the hay with you is like truth serum to a man: "Did you say the truth turns you on? Oh! Okay! So I was with these midgets, right? And we pulled out these monkeys . . ."

Well, maybe he won't tell you all about the midgets and the monkeys. But he will be more willing to give you the truth if you're willing to put in the work it takes to get to it.

# 7

## PRESENTATION IS EVERYTHING

### Don't Let Your "Off" Day Be Her "On" Day

Nothing moves men more than your graceful curves, the softness of your skin, the shape of your eyes, and the pout of your lips—the way your calves look in a sexy heel, and the way you sway and glide across a room, everything on your body moving in a perfect, deliciously beautiful symphony. These things drive us crazy. It is, absolutely, the first thing we will notice about you—every single time.

We don't care about where you work.

We don't give a damn about how much money you make.

We don't care if you can actually string a whole sentence together, really—at least not when we're deciding if we're going to get your attention. (When it comes to picking a partner to have children with, we tend to get a bit pickier.)

All a man is concerned about when he first sees a woman is

how she looks, how she's dressed, and what she'll look like on our arm when we're strolling along. To us, these considerations say the following things about you:

## YOU CARE ABOUT YOURSELF

Say your skin is a wreck, your fingernails are raggedy, your feet look like you've been running marathons barefoot, your hairdresser doesn't even know your name anymore, much less style your hair, and your closet looks like it came straight from wardrobe on the set of an '80s sitcom. What does that say about you? Nothing nice, I'll tell you that much. To a man—hell, to anyone looking—it practically screams, "My face, my body, and my clothes are nothing special—completely unworthy of anyone's time and attention, even my own." However, a woman who clearly looks like she takes the time to care for her self—gets facials and manicures (or, if she can't afford to go to the spa, creates her own spa at home), applies makeup in a way that is natural and appealing, wears a hairstyle that is flattering and clothes and shoes that are stylish—makes a statement, "I really like me, and you should know by looking at me that I do." Men appreciate women who value themselves, because it generally means that those women are happy with who they are and place a premium on their self-worth. We don't mind telling you you're beautiful, for sure. But if we're going to be in a relationship with you, we don't want to have to be responsible for *you* liking you. That's way too much work for any one man to assume, and rather than imagine ourselves doing all that heavy lifting, we'll just move on to the woman who looks like she can handle caring for and about herself on her own.

## YOU CARE ABOUT HOW YOU LOOK IN A MAN'S EYES

Say you are the woman at the club in the dress that's a little too tight, the top that's a little too low-cut, the makeup that's a little too loud, the hair that's a little too big and obviously fake, and the platform shoes that are a little too high. Oh, you might draw some serious attention dressed that way. But I can guarantee you that the men who will approach you have made some simple calculations in their heads: two Long Island ice teas + three dances + a couple of half-planned, zero-effort dates = a hasty romp in the hay, without any commitment from me. That woman will have men throwing her into the "sports fish/ throwback" category so quickly her bedazzled hair weave will spin. Remember what I said in *Act Like a Lady, Think Like a Man* about the "sports fish"? She's the one who sends off the signal that she has absolutely no rules, requirements, or respect for herself and that we men can treat her any old way, with absolutely no effort to make our connection permanent or long-lasting. In fact, the only thing we'll see in that woman is a hint of desperation, extreme tackiness, and a flashing neon sign on her head that'll blink, "One Night Only!"—as in, once that night of fun is over, we don't have to be bothered with her ever again. The woman who dresses sloppy sends signals too: men will assume that (a) you are incapable of fixing yourself up, that you don't know how to make yourself look hot and, quite possibly, could have some hygiene issues; (b) you don't care how you look and you could potentially embarrass him if he's going to introduce you to his boys or his family; and (c) you keep a nasty house. None of these things are a turn-on. None of them.

The kind of woman we will notice and approach is a woman whose dress style is sexy/neat—which is more subtle than sexy/provocative and more engaging than just plain. A woman who looks put together and sexy—who showcases her assets without oversharing and who uses her clothes, hairstyle, and makeup to good effect—is the one who says to men, "I am beautiful, I am to be respected, and you can take me around your mother and your frat brothers without feeling uncomfortable or embarrassed."

## YOU'LL MAKE US LOOK GOOD

This is critically important to a man. It is one of the first things that will come into our minds when we see you—how will I describe her to my boys? How will she look on my arm at the business dinner? Or at a Yankees game? If I took her home to meet my family, how will they perceive her? In the first moments that he sees you, a man is sizing you up for the long haul—how you'll dress when he takes you to the park, when you go to a house of worship together, when you're out at the club or having dinner with his friends, when he takes you around his coworkers, including those who make decisions about his paychecks and promotions. We look at and evaluate everything, initially based on how you look. Without even being conscious of it per se, we are giving you the head-to-toe once-over—taking in everything from how you've fixed your hair, what your nails look like, how your clothes fit to what your calves look like in those heels and what your body would look like in its natural state. If you look good, we instantly start to think of you as someone with whom we might have a future, someone who'll be part of the equation going forward. We've assessed that you could be the perfect fit to help us satisfy the three things most important to a man: who we are, what we do, and how much we make. This matters because appearance is everything to men; perception *is* reality. This is natural. It's not taught or learned—it's innate. Every animal has something they use to make themselves look more attractive—to look like the fiercest, most beautiful of the pack: peacocks have amazingly colorful feathers; lions have bushy, fiery manes; and elephants have long, strong tusks. We men have money and stature—a nice watch, a fancy car, an enviable job with a title. And we have our lady.

A pretty, put-together woman helps us exemplify the three things that drive us and certainly helps validate our worthiness to the rest of the world. If you're on a man's arm, looking absolutely stunning, well put together, and poised, then everyone is going to be looking at you and him and wondering, "Well damn, what does *he* do for a living? He must be all that." In the world of men, that's an absolutely necessary ego trip, one we cannot live without. Most women I know like retail therapy when they're feeling kind of blue. We men need ego therapy. And a stroll with a woman we perceive as beautiful can be as powerful a feeling as hitting the game-winning home run.

*A* woman who cares about herself and how she presents herself to the world, and looks like she'd elevate our game, is the woman who will get our attention; she's the one who will make a man down a shot, pat his boys on the back, and then take what feels like a twenty-mile walk through a crowded club to ask you for a dance, or work his way over to the vegetable section in the grocery store to strike up a conversation about the difference between Roma and vine-ripened tomatoes just so that he can talk to you.

Before you get too bent out of shape about what I'm saying here, keep in mind that this philosophy was taught to me by my mother, who dressed whenever she left the house—and she did this even though she was married already. It was she who taught my sisters to fix their hair and put on something nice and apply a little makeup on their faces before they left the house no matter what—even if they were going to the store for a pack of gum, it was important for them to step into that store looking "dignified." "Conduct yourself with some dignity so that at least if you see a man, he can say to himself, 'Wow, that's one dignified lady.' At least he'll know up front he's dealing with a person who cares about herself." The way you dress is an extension of you. If you're seriously open to a relationship, why miss the opportunity of meeting someone because you didn't pull it together before you left the house? I'm telling you, a single woman who is serious about finding a man can't afford days where she totally lets it all go. In the event that Mr. Right is somewhere in the vicinity, you have to be prepared to look the part of Mrs. Right. And if you're not looking the part, a man will not imagine you in the part either.

Instead, he might just turn his attention to the woman who did bother to go to the grocery store with it a little bit more pulled together. Your "off" day may totally be her "on" day— and in that split second when a man sees the two of you and is deciding which woman he's going to approach, I promise you that the one who's on her game will get noticed first.

Every. Single. Time.

So why not put into practice one of my favorite slogans— one I live by: It is better to be prepared for an opportunity and not have one than to have an opportunity and not be prepared. This is no different from the way you present yourself, say, at work. An employer will base decisions about how much you make, where you sit, what your title will be, and whether or not you get to represent the company in public based not just on your work ethic and how much you contribute to the bottom line, but also on how you look. You know this is true. He's not picking the employee in the frumpy suit with the greasy, unkempt hair and the chronic halitosis to sit in the board meetings or give the big speech at the shareholders' meeting; he's going for the employee who spends at least some of his earnings on a few quality suits, a prime haircut, a consistent manicure, and a generally strong appearance to be the face of the company—to be the one who best represents the image the company wants to put forward. That boss doesn't want anyone looking at his representative and drawing a bunch of bad conclusions, all based on one person's appearance.

I was explaining this point to my employees just the other day when I noticed a few of them dragging into work looking a little less than professional. I explained to them that even if they had a bad night or early morning, I shouldn't be able to tell it by the way they fixed their hair or the outfit they chose. I am not supposed to know they are going through a rough patch based on how they present at the office. I get that things may not be perfect at home—I understand that things happen and maybe you weren't feeling the business suit and heels and felt more in a jeans-and-sandals state of mind, but that kind of attire has no business in a professional setting. We have an image to uphold. I don't care how tired I am, I'm going to dress and make sure I look good. I'm not coming out of my house in a jogging suit, without shaving. I cannot afford to be disheveled, ever.

Because someone is always watching.

The same goes for women who are open to a relationship: you cannot afford to go to the party in a jogging suit, looking unkempt, if you're serious about finding a man. I'm not saying you have to hit the grocery store in a gown and chandelier earrings; I'm not saying that at all. But when you step out, step it up. Presentable does not mean perfection, but you can at least look pulled together. It's just natural that doing this will catch a man's eye—make him decide whether he's going to throw his bait your way.

Mind you, the need for you to look good extends beyond

the initial meeting and first few dates. If a man is still in the process of trying to determine whether he wants to commit to you, you can't just go au natural early in the relationship. You have to take it slow for a guy—leave the rollers, housecoats, and bare faces for when he's *really* into you, or else you run the risk of giving him an easy excuse to make a hasty getaway. If you want to extend the shelf life of the relationship, keep it pulled together long enough to figure out if the two of you have a chance together (and if you're following my direction, you'll be using at least ninety days to figure that out, right? Right!).

I have a friend who was dating this woman who appeared to be the absolute total package when he met her—when it came to looking good and the way she carried herself, she had few rivals. This was confirmed for my boy on at least three dates with this woman. After the third date, she invited him over to the house for a more intimate one-on-one date—just the two of them.

Well, when he went over to her house, she opened the door in house shoes, she had holes in her socks and a beat-up pair of sweatpants on, her hair was pulled back, and she didn't have on any makeup. She was in the house cooking and as she did so she said, "I figured we're just chillin' today and we should be relaxed."

"It just killed my whole image of her," he said. "I wasn't ready for that."

And who could blame him? Let a man fall in love before you show him the "real you," because like it or not, he's not about to find the sweatpants and the holey socks, or the woman who would reveal all that so early in the relationship, attractive.

Sometimes, I think you've convinced yourselves that if we are really into you, we'll accept you as you are from day one. "I'm going to show him the *real* me!" Well, he doesn't need to see all of that. You don't need to let out all the secrets—you don't need to tell him you were in the salon turning that chestnut brown hair blond and that those aren't your real eyelashes and the Spanx were the key component to that slick dress you were wearing when you first caught his eye. Let him develop deep(er) feelings for you before you start exposing the tricks of the trade.

My wife, Marjorie, whom I reconnected with and married twenty years after we met and briefly dated, effectively put this into play when we first started dating again, and I respected her for it. For the first five or six months of us being together, she always pulled it together—even when we were together in private. If she took a nap, she would wake up and head into the bathroom to freshen up before joining me. This sent a strong signal my way because any woman with a guy in my position is going to be in the spotlight, too, and by doing little things to always be on point when it was just the two of us, she demonstrated to me that she could handle this role were our relationship to deepen. The same holds true for every guy—not just a celebrity whose mate's picture will be in magazines. Every guy earning a paycheck does this because at the end of the day he needs to have a lady on his arm who will make him *feel* as if he's doing well (or at least better than he really is).

Of course, Marjorie is a lot more relaxed now that we're married, but in our house, even several years into our marriage, she'll only go so far with the au natural look. She'll pull her hair into a ponytail, but her skin will be glowing and her manicure and pedicure will be fresh. And she never goes out of the house—even for the simplest errands—without looking stylish.

I get that not every woman is going to want to get dolled up from head to toe every time she looks at the front door, but can you afford *not* to? Because let's not forget there is competition out there. And *she* will work it; everything from her hair and outfits to the shape of her body to her pedicure will be together. And when a man sees that, he's going to be attracted to her.

Now, we're not so simple that we're going to let go of something meaningful just because somebody else comes along and looks good. But if a man is still in the decision-making stage—he hasn't professed his love for you, hasn't done any real providing on your behalf, and isn't willing to protect you at all costs—don't give him a reason to walk away. This is something you can control; if he chooses to walk over and speak to you and ask you out and then ask you out again and again, then obviously, you're doing something right. Don't get too comfortable too soon and give the competition a leg up on your potential mate.

Even when you're in a relationship, you want to be careful; there are just some things you have to do to keep up the attraction you and your man have for each other. For sure, this goes both ways: no man should think it's okay to get too lax in the keeping-it-together department, and at the same time, expect his mate to be pulled together 24/7. I still dress up for my wife, and we're well into our marriage. Even on my casual days when I'm enjoying some downtime during the day, I put on a nice shirt and some slacks, shave, and freshen up before I come down for dinner. I do this because I don't want her to always see me onstage looking dressed up and jazzy, and at home overly casual and beat down. This is a good attitude for all men to have, but it's especially critical for men's wives and significant others. I told you in *Act Like a Lady, Think Like a Man* that the number one reason men cheat is because there are so many women willing to cheat with them. I say to you now that what you cannot do in your house is keep providing reasons for your man to keep looking somewhere else for aesthetic stimulation. I'm sorry but we men have to have it. It's what we like and we want it consistently. It simply isn't cool for you to get too comfortable, to show up at dinner in a head scarf, house shoes that date back to college, and sweatpants. We don't want to inhale the heady brew that's part cold cream, part nail polish remover when we snuggle. What we saw this morning when you left the house was a nice dress, pumps you convinced us were essential, though they cost as much as a weekend getaway, a natural but shiny lipstick, and a cute hairdo. We smelled the perfume in the air. We saw the smile on your face and the pep in your step when you hauled all that pretty into the office. We watched all of that walk out the door, but then got none of it when you got home. This might not be a problem for you if we weren't sitting in the office all week long, looking at all of our female coworkers dolled up and glamorous, looking and smelling good, only to come home to plain Jane. There could easily be a situation for you and your man if you let the other woman keep having her "on" days while you fill his days with nothing but "off."

Don't shoot the messenger just because you don't like the message but I have to ask: How long do you think that's going to fly with a man? You can get mad with me all you want to, but the idea that after a certain point, a man should just love you for who you are without some razzle-dazzle is not feasible in the real world. We know you give it your all at work and then come home and give your all to the kids and keeping the house together—we get that. But you've got to recognize what coming home to a woman who cares about her appearance does for a man—especially when we know you're doing it for us. Go home every once in a while and tell him, "You know, honey, I thought it would be nice for the two of us to come to the dinner table dressed up tonight—just for us."

Do that and suddenly the women dolled up at work aren't so special, because he's got dazzling at home. We know when you put on that sexy pair of underwear and that fitted T-shirt or that special piece of lingerie and you wait until the lights are out to tie down your hair that you're doing it for us, and we get a kick out of that. Do this, and you'll go a long way in keeping your man's eyes where they belong—even after you've fallen in love and, over time, your body has gone through physical changes. When we truly love you, we don't care that you're not the same shape that you used to be; you're still beautiful to us. While aesthetics is the number one reason why we approach you, it's not the number one reason we fall in and stay in love with you. We get the changes. We simply don't want you to let yourself go. We want to see that even with the changes, you're making the effort to look good—to turn us on in the same ways that you did when we met you.

Lord knows we're not going to stay the same guy you met; we'll have the potbelly or the bald spot, and body parts won't function like they used to, and even with that, you'll still love us. But that's no excuse for us to let ourselves go—to force you to feel like you have to continue Level 10 sexual attraction to us when we know good and well we look like we're barely on the deserving end of Level 5. Perhaps what we can both do is help each other get the sexy back—encourage each other to be better about living healthier lives, acknowledge and accept the changes our bodies go through as we get older, and help each other accentuate the goodness that's still there. You can find a hairstyle that fits a face that might be a bit bigger; he can find clothes that suit his changing body. The two of you could get into a great couple's exercise routine—take a salsa class together, or go for a brisk couple's walk after dinner—that will help you lose weight *and* connect with each other. Just making that effort together will go a long way in putting some pretty new bows on both of your packaging.

# PART III

## Keeping a Man

# 8

✦━･━✦

# THE COOKIE

## More on Why Men Need It, Why You Should Keep It

I mean, we just need it, man.

Like the earth needs the sun, like sharks need water, like Parliament needs George Clinton, Bootsy Collins, *and* Funkadelic, like Benny needs the Jets.

Men absolutely cannot—I repeat, CANNOT—live without sex, or what I often refer to as the cookie.

If he's breathing and free and clear of medical issues that would preclude him from getting some, then a man is going to have sexual intercourse. Period.

There is nothing on this planet that makes him feel better than sex. Not a hole in one on the golf course. Not a game-winning three-point basket at the buzzer. Not even the best drug. Hands down, it is the most gratifying, tension-releasing, confidence-building, conquering feeling any one human male could ever experience—the mere release is like a pressure valve being turned and all of that steam and buildup and energy rushes through, making the machine right again.

And in order for our machines—our bodies, our souls, and our minds—to be right, we're going to have sex by any means necessary. We enjoy the act that much.

What women have to understand, however, is that it is just an act. As clichéd as it may sound, men have nary a second's thought about separating the act of having sex from making and being in love. Of course, the more skilled our lover is, the more enjoyable it is—and if she's as beautiful as the ideal woman we've conjured up in our mind when we're fantasizing, it's all the more enjoyable, especially if she knows what she's doing. But really, we have no problem having sex, and hitting the road the second it's over. If we're not in love with our partner, we don't want to cuddle. We don't want to touch. We don't want to talk and share and emote and plan and dream with you. And if we do submit to the postcoital cuddle and conversation, it's most likely insincere—just a way for us to keep alive the possibility that if we need another sexual release in the future, you'll be available to us.

Cold but fact. Straight, no chaser.

Which is why we men never understood this whole concept women have about using sex to deepen a man's feelings for them. If you think because you have a special way of handing out the cookie that there will be a difference in how we respond to you emotionally, you're sadly, pitifully mistaken.

He just took the cookie because you passed it out. I'm serious. No matter how sweet and seductive you were, no matter how much you'd worked out in your mind that sleeping with that man was going to connect the two of you in ways that going out to dinner and a movie followed by a long deep discussion on a walk through the park never would, he was likely saying in his mind, "Well, I'm here, 9:30 on a Tuesday night. If we are efficient enough, I'll still be able to catch the sports highlights on ESPN. 'Let's get on in here, girl!'" Often, the physical connection doesn't lead to much more than that.

This is why I insisted in *Act Like a Lady, Think Like a Man* that women adopt the Ninety-Day Rule—a probationary period of sorts where you forgo having sex with the new guy until you figure out whether he is really into you or is just trying to hit it and quit it. I tell you, this was the chapter that women across the land gave me the hardest time about; all too many refused to even hear me out on this one. I had women calling into my radio show saying, "I don't know, Steve— ninety days just seems so arbitrary!" At my book signings and lectures from Brooklyn to Los Angeles, from Detroit to Topeka, and everywhere in between, women kept protesting that ninety days seemed "too long" and insisted that it's okay to do "what feels right" and "hope" that they wouldn't get hurt in the process. My personal favorite was a proclamation by one woman that she wasn't going to be bothered with the Ninety-Day Rule because she tried it with a guy and "he ended up dumping me because I wouldn't put out." As if that guy would have stuck around if she would have just given him some cookie up front.

I said it before and I'll say it again: the man who refuses to give you time to investigate whether he's worthy of intimacy with you is *not* your man. He's taking off because he doesn't have what it takes to meet your standards and requirements, isn't demonstrating that he's interested in what it would take to make *you* happy in a relationship. He's not looking to get emotionally invested in you; he's not even considering it as an option. So why would you want this guy to stick around?

Treat sex as if it's something special and let the man you're interested in know that it's special, and guess what? He'll either leave—which is what you want this guy to do if you're in the market for a serious relationship—or he'll see something special in you and do what it takes to meet your standards and requirements. When you require something of a man, he will have no problem giving it to you if he truly wants to invest in a relationship with you. Your prize is only special if you make us treat it as if it's special—if we are forced to say to ourselves, "Oh, wait—I can't just run up in here and get the cookie like I can everywhere else because this is more than just a hit-it-and-quit-it kind of girl." Men don't mind having to prove themselves, and you are worthy of the effort and the attention.

If, however, you're treating sex as if it's just a box of Chiclets, we'll run through the relationship with you as if it's a box of Chiclets. You know you don't chew Chiclets too long. You pop one in your mouth and you chew it for a little while and then you spit it out and get you another piece until the box is empty—until there's nothing left. You don't want to be the used-up, empty Chiclets box.

You want to be the one he feels emotionally connected to, because when a man loves you and he's committed solely to you, sex means something wholly different; now it becomes the pot of gold at the end of that rainbow. That ideal woman we've had in our mind since we became sexually active is now an actual person—our ideal woman personified—and when we have sex with that woman, our physical, emotional, and mental desires synchronize and work together to give a pleasure trip that is exponentially better than any other sexual experience we could ever conjure up in our mind, let alone ever have had. When we're making love to a woman we love, we don't ever want it to be over; we want to keep touching her and smelling her and drinking her in because every inch of her arouses us in ways that no other person can—drives us crazy, damn near. Sex with that woman rejuvenates us—gives us the strength to carry on, the comfort we need to continue, the feel-good we have to have to make it through the hard times. And we actually care deeply that our lady feels the same way about us and will aim to do whatever it takes to bring her that immense pleasure, because we love her and want her to feel what we feel. We want her to be happy.

Now men—and only men—can determine whether they love you and that your pot of gold is special to them. You can't decide it for a man—you can't say, "I'm going to get my sexy on so much so that he'll be too strung out to leave," and expect that it'll work. Trust me when I tell you, no man on this planet will make that determination without first being shown how *you* want to be loved, how *you* expect to be treated, and whether or not it's worth pursuing you beyond a casual romantic fling.

Ask any man living if I'm telling the truth and he'll tell you the same.

## COMMITTED SEX VERSUS FLINGS

Of course, even if a man is in a committed relationship with a woman he loves, sex is going to wane. That's just human nature. You're going to get comfortable with each other. I've yet to meet a parent of a toddler who doesn't find the king-size bed that was so immense during the honeymoon feels cramped when Junior starts walking in during the middle of the night (how romantic can that be?). Bill time is going to come around too often and with it the kind of stress that can play a number on your sexual energy. And somewhere along the line, there will be days when you're just going to be tired of looking at each other, even though you know good and well you can't live without each other. But even with all those changes, the one thing that I guarantee will remain constant is your man's desire for sex. Again, unless there is something physically precluding him from achieving intimacy, a man is going to want to have sex regularly, especially if he's committed to you.

Now I'm not saying he has to have it every night. That's for the young boys who don't have anything else to do but prowl for the next conquest. And I'm not suggesting either that a guy won't make allowances for natural occurrences that throw you off from giving us good loving, like illnesses and pregnancy and the like. Men are not heartless—we're not the dogs you make us out to be. But the release we get from sex is essential to our existence. As I've written elsewhere, it recharges our batteries, feeds our ego, releases a bit of the pressure cooker tension we feel. So if we're not getting the attention we need in the bedroom on a fairly regular basis, there's going to be problems. I'm not saying he's going to cheat. I'm certainly not suggesting that he has the right to cheat. But the temptation will certainly be there, and trust me when I tell you, it will cross his mind.

Of course, not every man is going to act on this. But those who do stray from a committed relationship to have a one-night stand are telling the truth when they say "she didn't mean anything." In most cases, *she* probably doesn't. What does matter to a man who chooses to have a fling outside of his committed relationship is that someone out there is willing to engage him in the thrill of the "chase and capture" men crave, and someone will give him sex with no strings attached. He's having sex with someone he doesn't have to argue with, someone with whom he has no responsibilities—they're not divvying up bills and raising kids and plotting out social calendars and building a life together—and someone who represents a nice little escape from all of the stress he's dealing with day in and day out. She dresses up for the occasion, makes the sex downright erotic, and fulfills whatever fantasy a man has worked out in his mind—the fantasy he can't get at home.

Once he's done with her, he'll be on his merry way—satisfied that he's recharged and can go on back to his real life with the woman he loves. Sex with that other woman is just that—sex. The other woman may not recognize or want to acknowledge this, but in most cases, it's the truth; and deep down, she knows it too.

Is a man wrong for doing this, knowing that even though sex with another woman means nothing to him, it's everything to you? Absolutely! Though every man who steps out on his committed relationship may have a pocketful of excuses for cheating, he knows really, there is no logical, acceptable, spiritual, or reasonable explanation for his actions, and that getting caught could mean the end of something beautiful. Every man eventually comes to a point in his life where he realizes nothing is worth losing his family—that the beauty of loving a woman, building a life with her and their children, being responsible for their care and well-being, and working with her to realize their dreams is more important than any orgasm he can have with another woman. A moment of pleasure for your life—that's a pretty high price to pay. The sad part is that there are a lot of cheaters who need to make the mistake, get caught, and pay that price before they realize the worth of what they could end up losing.

And that's the real shame of it all.

I'm not saying that in order to get your man to keep it at home, you have to drop and give him twenty whenever he taps you on the shoulder. A woman has every right to expect her man to be faithful—to expect that he won't end up in someone else's bed just because things aren't perfect at home. It is not your job to coddle and coax a man into being faithful; you can't change him if that's who he is. But like I said in *Act Like a Lady, Think Like a Man*, you can bring out the best in him. The two of you need to sit down and figure out together how you're going to make this thing right—how the two of you are going to work out how to get back to happy—and satisfaction—again.

I fully admit that when a man gets comfortable, he can forget what it took for him to have the honor of being your lover. He can slack off on living up to your standards and requirements—forget to buy you flowers just because, or neglect to compliment you on how beautiful and sexy you are, or think it's okay to lean on the quickie instead of putting in the work it takes to get you excited about sex. Men certainly don't teach one another that in order for a woman to be everything a man needs, he has to fulfill a substantial amount of her needs. He doesn't necessarily realize or remember that she likes to talk about her dreams and ambitions, or that she really liked it when they went out for dinner. He doesn't know she's sitting in her cubicle, listening to her girlfriend cooing into the phone, "I love you, too, baby," when Valentine's Day comes up and that while her girlfriend is getting a lot of things from her man, his girlfriend or spouse is upset that she's gotten a whole lot of nothing from hers. He doesn't know that everybody in the office is starting to question if she's even got a man, because he's never come in to take his lady to lunch or sent her a text message that made her giggle out loud or done something for her that's made her brag about him to her coworkers. Indeed, we men sometimes create the distance without even knowing it because we're so busy going about the business of manhood. How do you remind him? Talk. Most times it's that simple.

We men really are simple creatures and are almost robotic in our habits. As I explain in Chapter 12, "The Art of the Deal," if you tell us what you want, we'll do it, especially if it means we're going to benefit from it. If you tell a man he would get more sex from you, the woman he adores, if he made room for a once-a-week date night without the kids, or sent flowers just because, or chipped in more with the evening routine so you have more time to relax and get ready for him, guess what your man is going to do for you?

Similarly, if you're reluctant to have sex with your man because, well, he's not giving you something you can feel, then you're going to have to speak up. I promise you, he won't know you're not satisfied if you don't say it. Of course, each man is different, but we're all the same in one regard: we have tremendous egos when it comes to sex. No matter how good or bad we are, we all think we're bringing it—think we are doing the most to make you climb the walls. We think we're doing more than an adequate job because the work we're putting in, we've got nothing to compare it to. (No, porn doesn't count because we are not watching the guy—we're focusing on the woman and her reactions to what's being done.) You all have had lovers in your life and you can talk to your girlfriends about them and give them details—"girl, he kissed me this way and he rubbed me that way and ooh, he just wore me out!" But we men? We don't share that with each other. Ever. We can't turn to our fathers and ask them for advice because anything they tell us is going to automatically make us summon up images of them with our mothers and that's not an image a man wants to conjure up. Ever. And we don't talk to our boys about it at any great length because admitting we're low on techniques makes us weak in our boys' eyes and plus, none of us want our boys getting even a remote picture in their mind of our private parts or what it must be like to have sex with our women. So we're not learning from other men, either. Ever.

We learn from trial and error how to please a woman. We keep a mental Rolodex of what worked with each partner we've been with—"When I was doing that right there, it brought on a tremor . . . let me mark that one down," and "When I touched her there, she got excited . . . let me mark that one down." Once we've taken notes on the little spots, areas, and tremors that got our partners sexually aroused, we call ourselves experienced.

Nobody else we've been with told us we suck, and you're not saying anything, and we're always reaching our moment (whether you really reach your moment or not), so hey, we're killing! Every muscle on us is tight, we're shaking, the hair on the back of our necks is standing on end—we're good. Outstanding! So unless you tell a man you want something different, you're going to keep getting a whole lot of what you've already gotten.

Still, you have to be careful of how you ask for what you want. Like I said, men have tremendous egos when it comes to sex, and if you start with an attitude, "You know what? When you're with me, you're not doing the things I like," feelings are going to get hurt—not necessarily just his. And whatever you do, don't make a big production out of it. I told you in *Act Like a Lady, Think Like a Man* that the four words that scare the crap out of men and put them on the defensive are "We have to talk." So approach the conversation strategically—delicately. Be smart about it. The best time to bring it up is while we're in the actual act because when we're having sex, we're receptive to anything. If you say, "Baby, dive off the armoire!" he'll take his behind right on up there. If you say, "Oh, I love it when you do that right there," and "Ooh, turn me over now and go to the left, yeah!" he's going to do exactly as he's told.

You also have some other amazing tools to help you get the best out of your man; there's text messaging—"Honey, if you help me out with the kids tonight, at around 9:30 when they're in bed, we're going to be in bed and . . ." Put a sticky next to his shaving kit: "Remember when you did that thing to me? Ooh, I was just thinking about it and got shivers! Can you do that to me again?" You could always call his cell phone and leave a message: "I love it when you talk dirty to me—when I get home, I want you to whisper some dirty things in my ear and touch me there when you do it."

Over the course of two weeks, you can tell him everything you want him to know about what you like and get it. Because he's getting what he wants—great sex with the woman he loves—and he's pleasing her, making her happy. Which is all a man who is truly committed and in love with you wants to do.

We want to please the woman to whom we're committed and emotionally connected. We *really* do. Because if the two of us are pleased—sexually, emotionally, mentally—well, there's no way we're going to step out on that. The chances of that happening go down to damn near zero, because what a man knows through experience is that all of those "hope diamonds" are really just quarters compared with the pot of gold he's got at home. He won't jeopardize that by doing something he knows won't mean anything to him, but everything to you.

And that brings me back to why it's so important for women to make sure that they exercise the Ninety-Day Rule—to really scope out a man and figure out if he's worthy of the cookie before you give it to him. If you're truly looking for a commit-ted relationship, this guy has to demonstrate that he's worthy of and ready for one. Giving him sex is not going to make him stay around—not for the right reasons, anyway.

And here's the incredible thing about women I don't quite understand: you know when a man is not feeling you yet you still give your all, you continue to try to make it work. Why play that game? Why not just weed out, up front, all the men you know are going to do nothing but cause you heartache and disappointment, and wait for the one who is going to do right by you? Please understand, he's out there. There isn't a man living who can do without a good woman. Most men *are* going to get married. One of them will marry you. A real man won't be able to fulfill his destiny as a man without you. How else is he going to have kids? How will he continue his lineage? He wants that legacy; if a man can't do anything else, he wants his name to live on. Even if his father wasn't around, deep down he knows he can be the one to fix that—to break the cycle and start the tradition and be thought of as someone special to somebody. That's why our parents were so giving and hardworking—so that we could have a better life than they had. I'm sure my mother and father are somewhere looking at me and saying, "That's our son. We done good."

I remember when they were living and we were sitting around the Thanksgiving table and I saw my father lean over and tap my mother on the shoulder and say, "Did you ever think one of our children would be on TV?"

"Not in a million years," my mother said. "Ain't God good?"

And my father said, "I guess He is."

That's all a man wants—to have someone be proud of him

and to be proud of somebody. It's critically important to a man. And women help bring that about. We can't have babies without you, we can't build families without you, we don't get to be the man of the house without you, we don't enjoy dreaming without you.

We cannot exist without you.

Granted, we are not taught this. No man sits his son down and says, "Son, you can't truly live without a woman." But a good man will profess to anyone listening that he can't live without *his* woman. For sure, when my mother died, my father told me one day, "Boy, I figure I'll just go on and get out of here now, because life without your mother—ain't nothing here anymore. I always knew that life wasn't nothing without her."

Seeing how depressed he was, I'd tell him things to try to cheer him up even though he'd lost the love of his life—the woman he stayed married to for sixty-two years. I'd say, "Wynton just got here—he needs a grandfather," and I'd take him up to see my son. He'd say, "I guess I can hang around for old shotgun a little while longer." But as soon as he'd have a moment of quiet—some time to reflect—he'd go there again: "I wonder if the Lord will let me see her just one more time. I'm ready to see your mama, even if it's just for one more time."

Three years after my mother died, my father passed on. He didn't die from any specific illness—cancer, a stroke, or a heart attack. He just coolly went to sleep one night, tired. His heart was broken, because he couldn't go on without the woman who completed him.

The principles I've laid out here are the same ones I share

with my daughters *and* my sons. My sons are not being encouraged to go out and "conquer" the opposite sex; instead, I'm talking to them about respecting the young women they date the same way they would expect another man to respect their sisters. I also talk to them about the effects sex can have on their lives and the lives of the girls they may decide to be with sexually—to understand that being thoughtless and careless about intercourse can have devastating consequences for everyone involved. Emotional, mental, and physical consequences. And, if she ends up pregnant, there will be lifelong consequences on their ability to live their best lives.

My girls are taught that they need to be very clear about what their standards and requirements are and hold the men they date to them. I tell them constantly, too, that they've got to be willing to lose in order to win—to be willing to walk away from the bad situation to get to the good one. I add that this is a very simple matter of mathematics: plug in the facts and see if this guy is living up to what you expect. You deserve to be happy. You deserve to be treated like a queen. You deserve to be talked to with respect. You deserve to be taken around and presented with respect. You deserve to know what it feels like to feel special. "Don't let anybody come along and treat you any other way," I tell my daughters, "because you can always come over here and get special treatment from your father until you can find the man who can treat you the way I do." And I seal that with the declaration that they absolutely will not find out any of that about a man if they sleep with him too soon. I've said elsewhere I'm not a relationship expert—that I'm an expert on how men think and I know this much to be true. When I and the men I know have been confronted by a woman who respected herself and held her future in such high regard that she made it clear that she deserved only the best and would settle for nothing less, we've had no choice but to take stock and treat her with due regard. She might not have been the one for us, in which case we moved on. But what we didn't do after she made her demands clear is try to run our games on her, just kick it until Ms. Right did come along. How could we? She wouldn't let us. Which means that ultimately, she had the power. And you do too.

## FIVE STEPS TO TURNING UP THE HEAT WITH YOUR MAN

1. Invite him somewhere tranquil to have a one-on-one talk—preferably where there is water. I find that I have the best conversations with my wife at the beach, where, if you look out as far as you can see, there is nothing but sand, which is the earth; ocean, which is water; and sky, which is the heavens. When those three things are present, you're dealing only with God's creations—and that's got to be peaceful. Nobody is fighting at the beach or, say, at a tranquil place like Niagara Falls. Not near the beach? Go to a water fountain in a public park, or do something as quick and simple as inviting your man to a candlelit bath. All of these things will put him at ease, rather than announcing, "We need to talk!" or worse, trying to have a conversation about what you need sexually from him in the heat of a battle.

2. Pay a compliment before you offer up criticism. If you start by telling him what's wrong, he'll get too disappointed, angry, or embarrassed to hear you when you tell him what he's doing right. So choose your words carefully; let him know what he is doing that brings you immense pleasure. He'll appreciate the compliment and make the mental note to keep more of that coming.

3. Be specific. Tell him what you'd like to see more of in your relationship physically, mentally, and emotionally in order to

reconnect in meaningful ways. Be sure to ask him what he would like more of, too, so that the conversation doesn't end up being one-sided. After all, neither of you are perfect. Acknowledging that there are things you could be doing better, too, will help open him up to receiving your list of (gentle) demands.

4.  Get confirmation from each other. This is a very valuable tool that helps you both be crystal clear on what it is each of you requires from the other. You might even start off the confirmations by saying, "Okay, I'm willing to wear lingerie to bed at least three nights a week; would you be willing to light candles and find some mood music before we touch?" or "I promise to be more attentive and spontaneous, and in exchange, you can leave the lights on when we get it on."

5.  Immediately put your promises into action. I mean head right into the bedroom/the backseat of the car/your mother's laundry room and do what the two of you said you were going to do. Nothing solidifies the conversation better than that—and you're guaranteed to get exactly what you were looking for.

# 9

## THE "N" WORD

### How to Get What You Want Without Nagging

As much as we love the cookie, as much as we need the cookie, there is one thing that, when we see it, makes us want to run the other way, no matter what flavor the cookie. NAGGING. You can be part Miss America, part Ms. Tollhouse but once you start nagging, we're simply not interested.

Oh, trust me on this: we can see it coming. You walk through the house and start circling around, looking here, there, and everywhere, getting more and more upset with every step you take. Maybe the garbage can is full and there is a little odor to it. Or your man just happened to put his dirty clothes next to the hamper, instead of in it. Or there's a pile of dirty dishes in the sink. Next thing we know, you're standing in the kitchen with your top lip curled and that look in your eye, attitude so big it practically blocks the television from the next room over. We're trying hard to concentrate on what LeBron is about to do to Kobe, but your whole demeanor makes us sweat harder than a bottle of ice-cold Corona on a sweltering, hundred-degree summer's day.

Clearly, we've done something wrong.

We have no idea what it is, mind you.

But we know we're about to suffer greatly for whatever the wrong is.

"So what, you were just going to sit and watch the game while all those dirty dishes sat in the sink?" you ask, seething, tossing glasses and plates and knives around.

"Sorry, babe—I was just watching the game," we say back. "I'll get to them in a minute."

"I don't need them done in a minute—I need them done *now*. You saw they needed to be done; how you could watch the game all cozy and comfy and leave this sink full of dirty dishes for me to do . . ."

And just like that, you're going from zero to sixty, talking all kinds of crazy at us. You know what's flashing in our minds? Your transformation into a big, evil monster. It doesn't matter how tiny you are or how cute you are; when you're ticked off and blaming whatever you're ticked off about on us and using that "I'm ticked off" tone, you become a six-feet-tall, 450-pound troll head with a Darth Vader voice.

You are no longer the woman we fell in love with or a woman we even like.

In fact, love isn't even in this.

Whatever words come out of your mouth, the translation in

our heads sounds a little like this: "So what you're saying is you want me to leave and watch the game elsewhere. That's cool—that's what I'll do. Maybe I'll call one of the guys, we'll meet down there at the sports bar. Or I could go have a beer at the park. Or sleep in the car. Or fix the lock on the basement door—yeah, lock myself down there, where there's peace."

When you're going off—whether it's with nasty words, aggressive actions, or the stone-cold silent treatment—we're responding either by checking out, spacing out, or arguing back.

No matter our response, you're likely not getting what you want.

So how, exactly, does going off on your man—the definition of nagging—help you?

Let me just go on ahead and tell you now: it doesn't.

No matter how good it feels to get it off your chest, no matter if you think what you're saying is justified, the fact of the matter is that when you talk sideways at a man, it makes it that much easier for him to dismiss you and your needs. He can justify his reaction based on your words and tone—you get loud, he can get louder; you throw out idle threats, here come a couple your way, with extra sauce on them; you give him the silent-but-angry treatment, he now can ignore you and whatever it is you're fussing about until he feels like the lady he likes is back again.

Until the environment is ripe for him to go into fix-it mode.

I wrote in *Act Like a Lady, Think Like a Man* how important it is for a man to simply fix stuff. We don't want to talk about it and ponder it and mull it over in our minds or argue the merits of it; just as communicating, nurturing, and listening to problems to understand them without any obligation to fix them isn't a man's way, neither is standing around and getting hollered at and screamed at over things we don't think deserve all of that energy, things that are not a priority to us.

Whatever the issue is, we simply want to fix it—without the ugliness and drama.

The key words here, ladies, are *priority* and *fix it*.

See, what is a priority to you may not necessarily be a priority to us. *You* may like the kitchen to be clean, or *you* may want the trash taken out as soon as the last paper towel makes the garbage reach the top of the bin, or *you* may want the lawn mowed on Friday evenings instead of Saturday mornings. But I can guarantee you that unless he's some kind of maniacal neat freak, your man is probably not focused on any of the things that are a priority in *your* mind. He's not holding out on washing the dishes or taking out the garbage or picking up his dirty clothes to spite you; he's simply not paying attention to it. Call it insensitive, argue all you want to about how he should know, by now, how much you can't stand these things, the truth is he didn't make these things a priority because dirty dishes, a full trash can, dirty clothes on the floor, and all of the other things that women tend to be particular about don't bother us. He might just have his mind on other things—things he considers bigger than a dirty glass or a full garbage can. Really, it has nothing to do with you.

So he left his dirty towel on the floor. Your man didn't do that to spite you; he just dropped his towel on the floor and forgot to pick it up.

So he didn't put the trash out on the curb the night before

the garbage man came. He didn't take it out just as he heard the garbage truck coming around the corner to spite you; he simply thought it didn't need to be on the curb until just before the trash man came through.

So he sat down to watch the game instead of washing the dishes right after the family ate the dinner you cooked. He's not waiting around, biding his time until you break down and wash them; he's decided to watch the game first and get to the dishes later.

In each one of these instances, your man had priorities that didn't coincide with yours right that minute. Or he may have done thirty-nine other things before you started yelling at him about the fortieth thing he didn't get to yet. For sure, he's going to get to the fix, just not on *your* schedule. How does that justify your turning into the 450-pound, six-feet-tall troll with a Darth Vader voice? In our minds, it doesn't. And your tantrums about these things are really received as nothing more than bratty behavior. So when you're finished swelling up and transforming and spinning and the argument is over and you're back to the cute, normal, sweet woman we like, we can fix what was wrong—wash the dishes, take out the garbage, pick up the dirty towel—and go back to what was a priority to *us*.

Now, we men get that our women are particular people with particular needs, and we're prepared to fulfill those needs. You just have to be more diplomatic about getting what you want from us. First, try to remember these five things before you go all in on a man about something you need done or don't like.

## 1. Adjust your tone.

Your man is not your child. If you're talking to us in that stern, accusatory, "I'm your mama" tone, like we're little boys, then we're going to square off like grown men. We have to stand up to that because you're questioning our principles. You're suggesting, in that motherly tone, that we're nasty creatures who don't care about clean houses, or that we're lazy creatures who sit around waiting for everyone else to do stuff, or, the most hurtful, that we purposely hold out on helping you because we don't care about or respect you. Of course, none of these things could be further from the truth. But as a result of your tone, now we're really not going to give you what you need or want the second you need and want it.

## 2. Let your man get to what needs to be done in his own time.

Sure, you may want it done right this second, but really? Is the sun going to stop shining if he washes the dishes during halftime? Is the earth going to fall off its rotational axis because he chooses to put his towel on the rack when he goes back upstairs in an hour, rather than right this minute? Is your heart going to stop beating because he left the mail out on the counter and made plans to file it after he got back from a round of golf? I mean, gold star for insistence, but the fact of the matter is that most of us already know you want the dishes washed and the towel up off the floor and the mail filed and we fully intend on getting to it. Just not right now. So hold your horses—exercise a little patience. Leave the kitchen and stop looking in the sink. Stay out of the bathroom if that towel is driving you that crazy. Don't worry about the mail. We'll (eventually) get to it.

## 3. Choose your battles.

If you're going from zero to sixty on every little thing, your man is going to automatically tune you out every time he sees the attitude coming. And I can assure you, when a man tunes out, he has a hard time figuring out when something's a not-so-big deal to you versus something that's a *really* big deal to you. For instance, if you're giving him a hard time every time he wants to play basketball with his friends on a Saturday morning, even when you know good and well that if he stayed home, he'd likely be right up under you, he'll be less likely to take you seriously on the one Saturday that you actually *need* him to stay home so that you can run to the office and put in extra time for a big meeting on Monday, or run an errand, or take some much-needed time with your girlfriends. All the fussing and nagging make him insensitive to the things that are really important to you. It's like the boy crying wolf; after a while neither your idle threats nor your nastiness are taken seriously.

## 4. Understand what's a priority for men.

There are some universal things that simply aren't a priority for most men: Housecleaning. Keeping the refrigerator stocked with healthy stuff. Attending PTA meetings. Making up the bed in the morning. Asking for directions. If we have a place to eat, sleep, and go to the bathroom, most of us don't necessarily care if the floors are clean enough for you to eat off them. And as long as there's beer and one or two things to suck down—a pack of hot dogs and some chips—we're happy with our meal plan. Who needs to go to the PTA meetings? We'd rather have our toenails pulled out one by one than sit around listening to a bunch of parents plotting out what color Kool-Aid to serve at the fifth-grade dance. Why make up the bed? We're just going to get back in it. And there is absolutely no way we're going to trot into the gas station and admit to another human being that we don't know where we're going. You know these things about us. Still, you expect us not only to notice when we need to stock up on more vegetables, make the bed, or go to the PTA meeting, but to be excited about them. Not happening. The universal truth of the matter is that this is how men are made. Women, on the other hand, generally have that magical ability to be attuned to their surroundings and the needs of others and to detect when something is wrong the moment there is a problem. You seem to absorb everything—to take it in, process it, and make sound decisions for everyone involved. Us guys? To hell with what needs to be done or what anybody has to say about it; we have the unique ability to block out what we consider minutiae. Think about it: Your child gets hurt and he goes to his father for comfort. What's he going to get? A fix-it solution: "Go over there and sit down until it stops hurting," the father will say. And that kid will look up at his dad with that look in his eye, like, "Dang, I need a hug, kiss my boo-boo, you need to blow on it or something!" That same kid goes to the mother and knows he's going to be nurtured, that she'll make it better, clean it up. Admittedly, this is a burden. It is your blessing and your beautiful burden. You all look at the painting and notice the brushstrokes and different shades of blue and how the texture makes the lady's eyes stand out, and all we see is a lady in a picture in a frame. The same applies with life: women are detail-oriented; men operate in broad strokes. This is not to spite you. It is what it is. Now, if something is a priority for you, you need to let us know that, or we won't treat it as such. I'll address later how you go about doing this, but the best way to get someone's priorities to synchronize with yours is to let him know the urgency and be genuine about it. If having the bed made is a priority for you, let him know it. He may not make it a habit to live up to your standards of having a made bed every single, solitary day, but chances are if he sees how important it is to you, most men won't have a problem putting in work to at least meet some of your needs.

## 5. Whatever you do, don't take over the tasks—especially with an attitude.

I promise you, the only person who gets bothered by this is you. Oh, you know what I'm talking about: your man is in the basement enjoying the game or maybe playing a little video game or staring into his computer and you're upstairs turning five shades of purple or red over his lack of enthusiasm when you announced you want the bed made and the floor vacuumed. Oh, he agreed to do it. But he's not doing it on your time schedule, so now you're in the bedroom, snatching the covers and tossing pillows and flinging vacuum cleaners all over the room, talking about, "I'll show him!" You know what you get from this? A made-up bed and vacuumed carpets that you pulled together on your own, and a level of anger that could easily give you a stroke. What did your man get out of it? A made-up bed and vacuumed carpets he didn't have to be bothered with. Your doing what you asked us to do doesn't bother us one bit, especially if we told you we're going to get to it. If you want it done when you want it done, then go ahead and knock yourself out—now it's done, problem fixed.

Of course, a smart man knows that he'll suffer greatly for this later on, but we don't get to this understanding easily. We'll come into the bedroom listening to you on the phone with your girlfriend, laughing and joking and having a good ol' time, figuring we're in the clear over that little dustup with you earlier that day. What we'll soon find out, though, is that the happiness is reserved for the girlfriends—you've actually put a little funky cloud in a box and wrapped it up all nice with a pretty bow, just for us. All too often, we fail to understand that we never win when we let you handle what we agreed to get done and should have gotten done, and if you're asking us to do something, it's likely for a good reason. So I admit it: we men could be better about handling our business so that you don't have to nag in the first place.

Yet given that we fall short, what would be most helpful in getting us to this mutual place of understanding is if you simply asked nicely and explained why you need something done not now, but *right* now. Think about it: When a man wants something from you—no matter what it is—do we ever come at you fussing? Have you ever heard a man say in a gruff voice, "Hey! I need these shirts taken to the dry cleaner this minute or there's going to be some problems!" or does he ask in a civil conversation for what he needs? We know this is the best way to get what we want; we already know not to push you, we already know not to talk down to you, we already know that's not the best way to get what we need from you, whether it's sex or permission to buy something or our preference for the family vacation destination. We always bring our requests to you in a nice fashion, and there's always some sound, reasonable explanation behind why we're asking. We're always going to come in the door correct each and every time—and we know that, mostly, we're going to get you to give us what we want willingly, just because of the way we presented it.

Master *that* trait.

I use it in my house all the time, even when I'm not getting my way. For example, I've called my wife and said on many occasions, "When I get home, be dressed because I got somewhere special I want to take you. I can't wait for us to spend a little quiet time together." And on every last one of said occasions, I've gotten home only to find that Marjorie is nowhere near ready to go. Now, it's been hours since I made the initial phone call—there was plenty of time for her to do her hair and get her makeup just so and find just the right dress and shoes to wear out. Still, I'm sitting in the room, tapping my foot and waiting. Now, if I were going to nag, I'd get a little bass in my voice and go all the way in: "What do you mean you need more time? How in the hell are you not ready? If you're not ready in five minutes, you can forget going out!" I know better. Hollering isn't going to get her to move any faster; the only thing it's going to get me is an argument and a dinner date so full of attitude I'll wish I'd never planned it in the first place. If I do, indeed, want the evening to go well and the goal is for us to go out and have a nice time together, I'm going to do what I need to do to get my wife to move a little faster so we can keep our table. First, I'll call the restaurant and push back the reservation because, hey, the goal is to eat out with my wife and make her smile—not eat at that very specific time I initially set. Then I'm going to go into the bedroom and say nicely, "Babe, you're not ready yet? I'm trying to surprise you—come on now, I really want to get you there. Hurry, okay?"

That line, delivered in a kind voice with logic behind it gets Marjorie to move (a little) faster. And when she comes down the stairs, she's going to be looking good, she's going to have a smile on her face, and she's going to say, "I'm sorry it took so long, baby, but I'm ready now," and we're going to go on off and have a nice time.

Instead of fussing at your man, try using that approach. Say, for instance, you have some friends coming over and you need help getting the house in shape, but your man is on the computer doing whatever it is that he does on the computer. He's not paying attention to the dishes in the sink, he's not noticed that the guest bathroom needs freshening up and the kitchen floor needs sweeping, he doesn't necessarily care that the TV room tables need dusting—until, that is, you start slinging stuff around and barking about how you "sure wish that people in the house other than me would help clean up what they mess up." Your coming at him firing gunshots is not going to make him dig right in.

If you want him to help you pull it together, go in and ask him nicely: "Babe, I got some friends coming over and you know if they see the mess in this house, they're going to call me out on my homemaking skills, so I really could use your help straightening up. I promise you after you hook me up, I won't bother you anymore." Your man is going to sign up for that, for sure, because he'll know that there's some urgency to the request and that you sincerely need help and aren't using anger to pass judgment on his abilities, question his cleanliness, or make assumptions about his upbringing.

You have to use what you got to get what you want (there's more on that in Chapter 12). Women are masters at this! You know the best way to get something out of someone is to be kind and sweet and ask nicely, and you also know full well that talking crazy to someone will get you nothing. Still, you rush in, guns blazing, trying to get what you want anyway—a move that makes you lose control over the situation and give up all of your negotiation skills. Instead, calm down, take a deep breath, and go in there and ask for what you want like you would if you were asking for something good—like a new designer bag. I guarantee you'll get better results than you will lobbing negative, harsh talk at your man. This approach won't change your man, but it surely will bring out the best in him.

Marjorie is quite good at this. I'll tell you this much: when we decided to move in together and get started on our journey through life with each other, I sat my girl down and made something very clear—I don't do housework. I have no problem eating and leaving my plate on the table to be picked up by someone else, and I've been known to climb out of my clothes and leave them laying on the floor. I pay professionals to keep my house clean. I admit that there are plenty of men who don't have access to housecleaners, but hell, I do. And so I told my intended that I would pay a gang of folks to do these things, just so I didn't have to and she, a neat freak, wouldn't have to be bothered by dirty dishes and clothes.

This, of course, didn't stop her from trying to get something entirely different from me. I'd eat dinner and push away from the table, and she'd say, "Steve, scrape your plate off and rinse it." I'd take off a shirt and drop it inside the closet, and she'd say, "Steve, you just dropped your clothes on the floor." And the whole time I'm reminding her that's what the housekeeper is for. I pay them good money to handle these things—provide a job to someone to clean the house. "You want me to help them do their job? Because they're not helping me do mine. They're not writing jokes and holding them up for me to read while I'm up on the stage, so let them earn their money. Cleaning is what they do."

Except on the weekends.

It's then that both my closet and the kitchen start to look chaotic, because the housecleaner isn't there to pick up the pieces. And I realized pretty quickly that piles of laundry on the floor, dirty dishes in the sink, and an unmade bed in the master bedroom affects Marjorie's mood. When we lie down on Saturday evening, she jumps up out of the bed, insisting, "I can't deal with this—look at this bed! It's not made up. I have to fluff these sheets and tighten up the corners . . ."

And now, Saturday night isn't what it's supposed to be because my lady is bothered by the sheets, she's thinking about the sink full of dirty dishes downstairs, and she's staring at the pile of underwear, T-shirts, and pants piled up in the corner. But instead of letting it fester, she simply communicated what she needed from me in order to be comfortable in our house when the housekeepers aren't around. She didn't throw a tantrum, she simply said, "Steve, it would make me so happy if you tried just a little harder to keep the house neater until the housekeeper comes back on Mondays."

It was clear that my priorities had to align with hers or there would be problems. But there was no nastiness accompanying the request. And I rose to the occasion. I'm not saying my wife changed me. But she did bring out the best in me—the concern that I have to make sure she's happy.

So instead of just dropping my clothes any old where, I pile them in a corner out of sight so that she can't see them so easily. I get out of the bed on the weekends now and I actually pull the covers up tight and put the pillows (all those useless pillows that have nothing to do with nothing) onto the bed. And I make the kids load the dishwasher so their mom won't trip.

Then Marjorie is happy. She has no reason to nag. And I don't have to watch my perfectly beautiful, diminutive wife turn into a 450-pound monster with a Darth Vader voice, which makes me equally happy. Of course, on occasion, we still have our issues, still have days when all is not perfect in the Harvey house. That's the nature of being human. But the understanding we have and the care we exercise to respect each other's boundaries, needs, and wants make life together pretty sweet—and nag-free.

# 10

✦—·—✦

## SHOW YOUR APPRECIATION

### A Little Bit of Gratitude Goes a Long Way

I was not expecting this—it caught me totally off guard. I wasn't even thinking about how to put a smile on her face. Mind you, I specialize in making my wife, Marjorie, happy: I love nothing more, other than God and the Lord Jesus himself, than to see Marjorie's beautiful eyes light up—to watch her smile spread from ear to incredible ear. But at that very moment, all I was looking for was a rare piece of quiet time in my comfy leather chair—no work, no nagging kids, no drama. Just me and a fine cigar.

There I am, walking past the living room, headed straight for some me-time when I overhear my wife on the phone, bragging to one of her girlfriends: "Girl, I'm so fortunate. My husband is always trying to do something kind for me. He doesn't have to do it, but he does it, and I appreciate him so. He works hard, he's kind and thoughtful . . ."

The little boy in me went, "Oooh, oooh, oooh! Wait! She's talking about me! I have to do something nice for her *right now* because she likes that!" And even as she continued her conversation with her girlfriend, I made a beeline to my office and got on the phone and hurriedly put in a call to her favorite florist. "Listen," I said, practically huffing from rushing to the phone, "I need an abundance of my wife's favorite roses at the house by four this afternoon." And before I hung up the phone, I was thinking up more ways to bring a smile to her face, just so I could get a little bit more appreciation from Marjorie.

The truth is nothing in the world makes a man square his shoulders and hold his head up higher than when someone shows him appreciation. We men have responded in positive ways to praise and appreciation since the moment we were old enough to understand the praiseworthy words coming out of our mothers' mouths: "Look at my little man, he's so strong!" would make us grab four more grocery bags out of the trunk of the car, just so that we could look stronger in her eyes; "My boy watches out for his mama—won't let me cross the street unless he's sure I'm safe" would make us cement ourselves on the corner and look both ways forty times before we let our mothers so much as hang her pinky toe off the curb; "My boy is such a man of the house—he locks up all the doors in the house before we go to sleep every night so nobody can get in here" would make us do CIA-worthy perimeter checks on the house every night to make sure the family could sleep soundly, without anyone having to remind us to do it. It didn't matter how puny we were or that we couldn't flick a flea without falling on our behinds, if our mothers praised us for standing tall, we would stand taller. Because her praise—her willingness to say out loud that she appreciates us—made us feel valued, which in turn gave us joy.

This need to feel appreciated is human. No matter if you're a husband or wife, boyfriend or girlfriend, or adult, teenager, or child, every last one of us looks for a stamp of approval and a simple thank-you when we lend a helping hand, get the job done, and especially when we get it right. But when you show that appreciation to a man, his response to it is immeasurable because men are so rarely thanked for what they do during the course of their days that when someone does extend a simple, "thank you, you are appreciated," they feel as if they've won the lottery. His boss isn't likely patting him on the back with a "Job well done." He's giving him a paycheck—that's thanks, enough. His friends aren't high-fiving him and saying, "You're a great friend, man!" We're way more casual about it, if we bother congratulating each other at all. And guess what? Rarely does that appreciation come from the women we love.

It is the latter that hurts men most. An admirer of the work of women, I get that no one can multitask like a woman, that you are *busy*; in many cases, you're working and may even be the breadwinner for the family, you take on the lion's share of the child rearing and the household duties, and you are the keeper of the family's social calendars. If left to men, the kids' annual checkups would take place every lunar year, that is, hardly ever; birthdays would never be celebrated and gifts never purchased; and there'd be no family vacations. Yes, you run the households the way corporations *ought* to be run. But often, husbands and otherwise committed men feel like they're near the bottom of their ladies' list of priorities, and the only time they get any kind of feedback from you is when they're not doing something right or falling down on the job. After a while, men can start to feel like they're being taken for granted—that no matter how much they do to help, no matter how much they're stretching outside of themselves to participate in the relationship in ways that aren't necessarily natural to them, it's never going to be enough to keep a smile on their ladies' faces. And when a man has spent the day getting dogged out at work, or facing off against the forces that conspire to bring him down, he wants to be able to turn to his family, and especially the woman he loves, for some uplift, a kind word or two that makes him feel like he was of some use to somebody today.

So when men get recognition from their women for getting something right, it's like they've broken the code to Fort Knox. It's as if they were stumbling through life, totally clueless about what to do to make the one person who matters most to them happy, only to discover quite accidentally that they've made the women they love smile *and* say "thank you." And once a man knows he's done something right, he'll keep doing it again and again—providing you with what you want—just so he can revel in that feeling that comes when he knows he's made you happy and you showed him appreciation for it. As I have said elsewhere, a man expresses his love in three ways—by professing his love for his lady, protecting her, and providing for her and the family they build together. His desire to profess, protect, and provide for you will only get stronger if you make him feel appreciated. Simply by saying thank you to your man, you validate his decision to provide for you and encourage him to keep expressing his love for you.

This is what I had to clue one of my friends, Gwen, in to when she complained about her husband, Rick, who began fishing for compliments after another mom praised him for helping get his young daughters ready for school in the morning. Gwen's friend thought Rick was amazing because her own husband played absolutely no part in the morning ritual while she fixed breakfast, ironed school clothes, packed the kids' backpacks, and got them off to the bus stop. "He barely looks up from his BlackBerry to give them a kiss as they're heading out the door," the woman told Gwen. "Your man is cooking eggs and ironing shirts and walking to the bus stop in the morning? I wish he would teach a thing or two to my husband and a few others, too!" she continued.

Gwen later told me that Rick jokingly stuck his chest out and said, "See? Barely any of the other fathers do what I do!" at which point Gwen went off on the situation. "He's supposed to help with the kids—they're his kids too!" Gwen snapped. "Nobody stands around applauding me for cooking dinner or doing the laundry or going to the PTA meeting; why on Earth should someone clap because he exercised some responsibility and participated in the care of his children?"

She has a point: she and her husband share the responsibility in raising the kids; this is true. But, I pointed out, it was unfair for her to assume that it comes natural to her man—heck, any man—to cook eggs and iron clothes and organize math homework in the morning in the same way a mother would. Maybe all of that is in your "How to Be the Best Mom Ever" manual, but I assure you that it doesn't say anywhere in the universal "Manual of Manhood" that men are *supposed* to get up in the morning and fix breakfast and get the kids off to school. Cooking dinner and changing diapers and running baths is not something taught to us by our fathers. We certainly didn't learn it from our mothers, who give plenty of nurturing to the boys, but save the "how-tos" of child care and nurturing for the girls. What does get hardwired into our DNA is that it's our job to work hard to make sure there's money to put food on the table, clothes on our children's back, and a roof over our family's head. We internalize from the earliest ages that everyday child care and nurturing is what women do, and if we put our hands on anything outside of putting checks in the bank and doing the more male-oriented things, like fixing the car or keeping up the lawn, then we're going above and beyond what is expected of us. And trust me: men are more prone to go above and beyond if you encourage them when they complete tasks that don't come naturally to them. I can almost hear the collective groans washing over these pages. I can picture you sucking your teeth and asking anyone who will listen why a woman has to applaud a man every time he does something right. As an entertainer, I know firsthand that there is nothing more gratifying than a round of applause. No matter what room I walk into—whether it's a comedy club where I'm about to tell jokes, a charitable dinner where I'm about to introduce an organization, or a church where I'm about to enjoy Sunday service with my family—someone is clapping for me, and I value it, because it tells me that somebody cares about the joke I'm about to tell, or the charity on whose behalf I'm about to speak, or the nourishment I'm about to receive for my soul. The recognition validates my performance and I'm going to try to duplicate that performance or do even better the next time so that I can get that applause again. If, instead of clapping, people get up and walk out while I'm talking, then I know it was a bad night.

Now wouldn't it be great if you could have that same feeling? What if you came in to work today and as soon as you walked through the door, somebody came on the loudspeaker and said, "Ladies and gentlemen, Jill is here!" and everybody stood up and clapped for you? What if you went down to the grocery store and just as you walked through the automatic door, someone announced, "Hey, everybody—a round of applause for Sophia! She's in the house!" Wouldn't that make you dress up a little nicer for work? Take extra care with your hair? Put on a little extra lipstick? Admit it: you would feel magnificent.

By the same token, your man would feel similarly uplifted if, every once in a while, you gave him a proverbial round of applause and recognized the value of appreciation.

Now, I understand this goes both ways. Like women, men tend to underestimate the value of appreciation too. We'll go from challenging ourselves to get you (calling and texting every two hours, sending flowers, taking you on romantic getaways) to getting comfortable after we got you (checking in instead of having a real phone conversation, buying flowers solely on special occasions, and vacationing only every once in a while), to acting as if our relationship is built solely on convenience (never calling, rarely giving gifts or vacationing, and expecting all the fixings that come with being in a committed relationship with a woman, including hot meals, clean homes, and well-cared-for children). And by the time we get to the "convenience" stage, we're not giving our women any credit or expressing any appreciation for all that she does for us, our homes, and our families.

In other words, men and women are both expert at taking each other for granted. We treat the everyday efforts we make on behalf of each other as commonplace—something as unnoticeable as our own heartbeats. But just like we praise God for waking us up each morning with the blood still pumping through our veins, we could stand to look our partners in the eyes and say, "thank you for all that you do."

Matter of fact, some women don't have a problem asking for that kind of recognition from their partner. How many times have you pointed out that it would be nice if someone said thank you to you for standing over a hot stove and cooking up three-course meals every night after a hard day's work? Or that there better be a romantic dinner planned for all the washing, drying, and folding of clothes that you did all weekend because if you hadn't done it, everybody would be going to school and work buck naked? I'm even going to go out on a limb and say you probably even uttered a silent "better had" the last time your man invited company into the house and expressed in front of his mother, father, sisters, brothers, and the family dog that he's eternally grateful to have married such an incredible woman. In your minds, men are *supposed* to show their appreciation—shower their ladies with gifts, tell them they're lovely, and very publicly sing their praises.

Yet no one seems to ever expect women to reciprocate that appreciation, even though we, too, provide things that are absolutely essential to our lives together—security, wealth, strength, and even the occasional diaper change, cooked meal, and folded load of laundry. Think about it: your man can go to work every morning, run the kids to soccer practice, put them to bed while you run a few errands on Wednesday evenings, run to get your prescription whenever you need it, bring home his paycheck every Friday, cut the lawn and barbecue dinner on Saturdays, and run you to church each and every Sunday, and not get a lick of gratitude. How is that possible when the teenager who packs your groceries and offers to walk them out to the car for you will get an Oscar-worthy show of appreciation—maybe even a little tip if he doesn't break the eggs—once he puts the bags in the trunk? In other words, someone does something nice one time, and you extend gratitude. Doesn't the man who regularly puts in work and *tries* to do the right thing for you and the family deserve as much? Tell him you appreciate him.

Your son's father may not get him ready for bed at night, but he may have taken him outside in the backyard to teach him how to line his fingers up just right on the stitches on his old football and throw it all the way past the tall oak. And the half an hour he spent playing with your son may have even freed up a half hour of quiet time for you. Your husband may not get up in the morning and get the kids on the bus, but I bet you he works hard to make sure the school tuition is paid or there is extra money for those baseball uniforms and ballet outfits. Tell the man you appreciate that. I guarantee you, not only will he be grateful for your noticing that he took the time, he'll be more likely to do it again, just so that he can repeat how it feels to be appreciated. Say, "You know, babe, I've always wanted my children to go to that school—thank you for helping to make that possible." Or, "John really wanted to play in that league. Thanks for making it possible." I guarantee you, this will make your man stick his chest out; it validates him—assures him that he's providing to you and your family the Three P's that show he loves you. He's providing that tuition, and he's protecting your child by making it possible for your child to get the education he'll need to exceed in the career he'll eventually choose. Isn't that worth a simple thank-you?

This will not come naturally; it's so much easier to keep your head down and your nose to the grind, getting what needs to get done, done. But if your relationship is going to survive, you're going to have to expect and demand that your man show you appreciation, and it sure would help the situation if you showed some to him, too. In the end, you might just get a little something for yourself in return.

My wife, Marjorie, has this down to a science. Take, for instance, the solo weekend getaway I was plotting just this past spring. I had it all laid out: I was going to check into a beautiful golf resort in Georgia sometime on Saturday afternoon, get in a golf lesson at 5:00 P.M., and spend the evening resting and enjoying a few cigars, and then wake up on Sunday, have a nice breakfast, rest up a little more, get in another round of golf at 3:00 P.M., and then head back home just as the sun was setting so I could get in some quality sleep before I dove headfirst back into my hectic work schedule. This was going to be a rare two days of uninterrupted downtime for me—no radio show, or business meetings or comedy gigs, no TV appearances or social functions, no press interviews or photo shoots. Just me, my golf clubs, and silence. Man, when I tell you how excited I was about this? You can't even begin to imagine.

Just as I was putting the final touches on my plans, Marjorie comes into my office, sits down in a chair across from me, and says, simply, "You know, Steve, I just love your spontaneity!"

"Really? What makes you think I'm spontaneous?" I asked, smiling.

"You're not just crazy, you're actually a lot of fun to be around, you take time to enjoy life. You like to make it seem like you're a homebody and you never want to leave the house, but I love that you're getting out, going golfing and fishing and doing the things that you love to do," she said sweetly. "I love that about you and I'm glad you're like that because it inspires the rest of us to enjoy life. That's a great quality to have in a mate."

Before she could get the last of her sentence out of her mouth, I had invited her to come with me on my solo golf weekend getaway. I mean, how could I resist? Here was this beautiful woman complimenting me on something I didn't even see in myself, and thanking me for leading by example.

"Wow, really? You want me to come with you on your golf weekend?" Marjorie asked, shocked by the invitation.

"Yeah!" I said excitedly before I could even think to stop myself. "And I'm going to take all the kids!"

Now, even as I'm extending the invitation, my brain is going, "No, dummy! That's not quality alone time! Those kids are going to be acting crazy, there's water and jet skis and they're going to want to rent a boat and you're going to have to do all of that with them and you can kiss cigar smoking, sleeping in, and those leisurely rounds of golf good-bye. What's *wrong* with you?"

Next thing I know, it's a family affair—all of us are headed to the lake on my *solo* golfing trip, just because my girl extended a thoughtful comment that made my heart swell. She wasn't trying to horn in on the trip; she genuinely was happy to let me get in my alone time. But it just felt right to bring her and the kids along because this woman was showing her appreciation for a characteristic I barely saw in myself.

And though I surely would have enjoyed spending that time alone, I had an incredible time bonding with my family. We rented a cottage, caught up with one another's lives, snuggled around the fire pit (making and eating enough s'mores to feed a small army), and laughed and played together way into the night. Marjorie got a massage while I hung with the kids, and then she spent time with them while I got in my tee time out on the golf course.

And when my caddy pulled up to the cottage after my golf outing, Marjorie and the kids had a surprise waiting for me that I'll never forget: right there on the sidewalk leading to the cottage was a big pastel chalk drawing designed by my family, just for me. In big, colorful bubble letters, they'd written out "Welcum Home Deddy" with the "e" drawn backward, and each of my kids wrote their names and what they want to be when they grow up. There was also a sprawling family tree with all of our names as well as the names of the grandparents, uncles, aunts, and cousins. And next to that were two huge signs that said, simply, THANKS FOR THE TRIP! and TO DADDY, THE HARDEST WORKING MAN IN SHOW BUSINESS, with a hand drawing of a microphone and a crazy picture of me. Up on the deck, Marjorie had the grill going, and the kids were all there, waving and laughing and calling out to me.

Grinning from ear to ear, I couldn't find the words to express how good that made me feel. This massive display of appreciation from my family didn't cost much or take up a huge amount of time; the chalk couldn't have been more than a few dollars, the drawings couldn't have taken more than twenty minutes or so. But I'll tell you this much: their words of appreciation, sprawled out across the sidewalk for all the world to see, were worth a million dollars to me. And their smiles? Priceless. It validated for me that everything I'm doing to profess, provide, and protect my family is not only necessary, but well worth it. Things like this make me want to work that much harder for them, to make sure that they've got everything they need, and certainly to give them a lot of what they want, too.

My caddy, a young guy in his late twenties, took in the scene and, as he handed me my golf bag, said, simply, "You're a lucky man—that must feel great. I hope I have this one of these days."

"Yeah," I said, shaking my head in wonderment. "Every man should have a family like this."

## EIGHT EASY WAYS TO SHOW YOUR APPRECIATION—AND GET A LITTLE SOMETHING FOR YOURSELF IN RETURN

1. If your man barbecues a meal for you or your family, compliment his grill skills, and, the next time you buy a cut of meat from the grocery store, tell him you know your cooking it on the stove just won't compare to what he can do fixing it up over a charcoal fire.

   **WHAT YOU'LL GET OUT OF IT**: A man who will happily grill Cheerios on an open flame if it means he'll get another compliment on his cooking prowess.

2. If your man cuts the lawn every week and trims up the hedges to keep the yard looking good, show your thanks by presenting him with a small rose bush or hydrangea that can be planted out front.

   **WHAT YOU'LL GET OUT OF IT**: A pretty flowering bush that'll make the yard look great and, every time either of you pulls into the driveway, you'll be reminded of your solidly rooted relationship. Plus, when the flowers bloom, he might just cut a few and put them in a vase for you.

3. If your man fixes the leaky faucet or changes the showerheads in the bathroom, show him your thanks by running him a hot bath later that evening.

**WHAT YOU'LL GET OUT OF IT**: Some quality alone time while he's enjoying some for himself, or, even better, a steamy bath for two.

4. If your man helps the kids into their pajamas and reads a story to them before it's time to kiss them goodnight, tell him that watching him bond with the kids is total husband porn and turns you on.

   **WHAT YOU'LL GET OUT OF IT**: Trust me: he'll put those kids to bed most every night and give them plenty of, um, encouragement to stay there if he thinks it'll result in some quality alone time with you.

5. If your man makes all the reservations and arrangements for the two of you to have a fun, relaxing time together, tell him you appreciate his initiative to plan much-needed alone time just for the two of you.

   **WHAT YOU'LL GET OUT OF IT**: You'll spark his spontaneity and inspire him to plan more date nights for the two of you.

6. If your man fixes your car or makes arrangements with the mechanic to make sure it runs smoothly, or even just simply takes it to the car wash or fills up the tank with gas, thank him for keeping your sole source of transportation in good running condition.

**WHAT YOU'LL GET OUT OF IT**: A working ride and a lifelong personal mechanic/car washer/tank filler-upper.

7. If your man washes a couple loads of laundry but leaves them for someone else (that would be you!) to fold, thank him for helping clear the hamper of the dirty clothes and invite him to help you fold them—together.

**WHAT YOU'LL GET OUT OF IT**: Not only help finishing up, but some quality time talking and laughing with the guy you love.

8. If your man runs to the grocery store to pick up a gallon of milk and some eggs and cereal when you're running low, thank him for noticing you were out of the essentials.

**WHAT YOU'LL GET OUT OF IT**: A man who will be more likely to make runs to the store because he sees the need, not because you begged.

# 11

## DOLLARS AND SENSE

### How to Handle Money Problems with Men

I t's like my father used to say: the best thing you can do for a poor person is not be one of them. That's because if a person in need comes to you for help—he doesn't have the means to feed, clothe, or shelter himself—there's nothing you can do for that guy if you're broke too. This makes all the sense in the world to most men because we're really clear that no matter how much we love our significant others and the families we create together, we can't live off that love. It can't pay the light bill. It doesn't send in checks for the mortgage. You can't drive it to the store or buy groceries with it. And no matter how much hugging is involved, it will not keep the people we love warm in the same way that good old-fashioned heat and electricity will. Simply put: we need money to provide the essentials for the people we love. And a man—a real man—

will move heaven and earth to make sure that he has it, so that the people he loves have it.

The ability to do this is at the very core of manhood. From the moment the obstetrician smacks our bottoms and tells our mothers, "It's a boy," we are expected to understand and respect the fact that one of the most awesome responsibilities we will have as men is to have a clear-eyed, laserlike focus on who we are, what we do, and how much we make, and to use that to make sure that the people we love are taken care of—that they want for nothing, even after we've taken our last breath. As I wrote in *Act Like a Lady, Think Like a Man*, being the chief provider in our lady's life is also one of the key ways we show our love for her and the family we build together. It's absolutely critical for a man to show his love in that specific way.

Imagine, then, the problems that can arise if a man can't get his family's money right. Let's say you get married and the honeymoon season is over. Now you're in the thick of living your lives together and, suddenly, the grind of paying bills is getting complicated—you've got a couple of credit cards that are past due, the money you had set aside for rent had to be used to fix the car, and you're a little short on the cash you need for the gas bill. Now toss some kids in there and watch your bank accounts get sucked dry. This scenario was complicated enough while the two of you were single and dealing with it on your own, but the frustration, embarrassment, and stress only multiplies when you have to go through those financial complications in front of and with someone else, and someone other than you is severely affected. Not to devalue how women feel in these situations, but I can tell you that this can wreak havoc on a man's ego.

This man, who vowed to love you beyond measure, can't show his love in the best way he knows how—by making sure he can tend to your most basic needs and even by giving you the things the two of you dream about as a couple—a nice house in a better neighborhood, good schools for the kids, a comfortable and safe ride, a vacation or two. Multiply that by a thousand if he actually loses his job—a scenario that's not uncommon in our current economy, where men are taking the lead in the numbers of workers who've both lost their jobs and remained unemployed. A man who isn't working not only suffers the blow of not being able to provide for you, but he also suffers the indignity of feeling as if he can't protect you: if he can't afford to pay your car note, then you're on the bus; if he can't afford the rent, he's going to have to move his family to a neighborhood that may not be as safe and where the schools may not uphold the standard you had in mind for the kids; if he can't pay the electricity bill, the family is about to be a little chilly come wintertime. All of these things can make a man feel as if he's failing to love you the way you deserve to be loved. Consider, too, that if he loses his job, he's taking a hit in two of the three cornerstones of manhood—what he does and how much he makes. And that takes a huge toll on his identity and dignity.

You know what comes next: The two of you face down tough times with more arguments over spending. He checks out mentally and emotionally while the two of you grapple with hard financial decisions. He's tense and a lot more anxious, his temperament is off. He is less romantic, can't even think about sex because his mind is on twenty-four-hour churn, trying to figure out how he's going to hoist his family on his shoulders and carry them through the financial mess in which he's found himself. Most men want to do what they're supposed to do and what's required of them, and the moment they can't, everything comes to a halt. I'm the first to admit that even now, as the primary breadwinner, I go into a shell if my family is feeling any kind of financial strain, and I don't pull out of it until I can figure out how we can resolve any setbacks. During these periods, I'm not as talkative, I'm not as romantic, I'm not nearly as caring or attentive. I'm off in the corner with a look on my face that says, "I've got something on my mind and it will affect me and how I interact with you until I fix it."

Now, it's nice when our women try to console us with the "I love you no matter what and we can get through this" pep talk—we appreciate you and thank you for your support and vowing to be with us 'til the end. In fact, we need that support. But it's not going to change things—not going to affect in any way our mind-set. The pressure is on us as men, and no matter how much you say you understand and are in our corner, you cannot begin to fathom the pressure on us to produce, particularly in a man's world. Witness us running into an old friend when we're financially compromised and you'll get a little taste of what runs through our mind at a thousand miles per minute: *He knew I was the CEO of that company that tanked or that I was working at that plant that closed down a few months ago, and now when he asks me what I'm up to, my answer has to be, "nothing." And when he asks me about you, I tell him, "It's all good," when he knows you must be concerned because things are tight now.* A woman's pep talk, no matter how heartfelt, won't shake the feelings such an encounter can set off. And so we retreat.

But there are some ways you can help draw us out while we recover and figure out how to get back up on our feet:

# 1. ORGANIZE YOUR MONEY AND GIVE HIM SOME CONTROL

A financial planner gave me this critical advice years ago: to really organize your money and help everyone in the house feel like they're contributing and benefiting from their paychecks, every couple should have at least four bank accounts. One is the household checking account—the one where each of you deposits your paycheck. This makes one large family money pool from which a portion, for most of us the majority of, pays all of your bills and the necessities that help you live from day to day—the car note, the electricity and credit card bills, the tuition, the mortgage. The second account should be a savings account that requires two signatures to move any of the money. This is both the emergency fund—the cash you set aside for a rainy day and the fund in which you can save for life's big expenses: housing, automobiles, tuition. It doesn't matter if you transfer from your joint checking account 10 percent, 20 percent, or just $10 dollars a month; the point is that the two of you are using it to save, with the intention of using those savings for emergencies. The last two accounts should be individual accounts—one for him, and one for you.

Those accounts comprise the spending allowances the two of you agree to keep solely for yourselves.

Having these four accounts allows you to pool your resources together and work as a couple to get your finances in order, while helping you maintain your individuality. In some families, the car note may be her responsibility and the rent and tuition his. Now it's all shared, even the child support. Now the two of you are linked together in a united financial front. In good times, that means the two of you are contributing as a couple toward the upkeep of your lives. In bad times, it's the perfect way to help your man feel like he's still got a handle on the finances, even if he's not bringing in as much. If he's writing the bills and the checks have his last name on them and he's making decisions about which payment takes priority (or at least he thinks he is) and the lady down at the cable company is addressing him with respect—"Thank you, Mr. Johnson, for your payment"—then he doesn't feel like someone is kicking him in the teeth every time a bill collector calls or another late notice shows up in the mailbox.

The pep talk that keeps him focused is the one where you tell him no matter who is putting what into the account, you need him to handle the money and keep the bills as current as possible—and that you trust him to do it. This goes a long way in helping him maintain at least some financial dignity while he works to get back on his feet. For the women who feel like this is handing over too much control, know that you still share the responsibility; the two of you still need to talk about the finances, no one can dip into the savings without checking in with the other, and the two of you still have your separate accounts that give you the autonomy you need for yourselves without any questions from your mate. If he wants to buy a box of cigars, he can dip into his individual account to buy them, no questions asked; if you want to get your nails done or buy a cute pair of shoes and you have the money in your individual account, he can't say anything about it. See? Everybody has some control.

Now, if your man spends frivolously, isn't taking care of business, and doesn't seem like he's remotely interested in climbing out of his jobless state, you've got a problem—and I don't have the book to help you with that guy. Rest assured, a man who isn't taking care of business is going against what I think are his natural instincts, and if you happen to be hitched to him in any way, you have the absolute right and power to walk away. Or you can hang in there—and good luck to you.

But the bottom line is that when you make the move to be with someone, from the get-go you have to play the game like you practice the game. If you have the hard conversations about finances and how the two of you handle bills and saving before you get in deep, and put into place this practice of handling money together in both good financial times and bad, then the sharing is going to work, even when something goes wrong, *especially* when things go wrong.

## 2. REMIND HIM WHY YOU FELL IN LOVE

We've already discussed that telling your partner you love him when the chips are down is something that, while appreciated, may ring hollow with a man who's down on his financial luck. But showing him you love him is something wholly different. My parents didn't have a lot of money, but they made it. And I've got news for you: you can make it too. All that history together, all the time you've loved each other, is worth preserving. Show him that by reminding him what made him love you in the first place—by focusing on the little unexpected things. Make his favorite meal, hold his hand, send him love notes. Do things as a family that don't cost money: rent a DVD, make popcorn, and have movie night; spread a blanket on the living room floor and have an indoor picnic; after dinner, take a family walk around the neighborhood; go swing on the swings at the playground; park your car by the airport and watch the planes take off and land; drive to the suburbs and look at the Christmas lights; learn how to play one of his video games, then challenge him to a duel. While you're out on those impromptu "dates," take care to enjoy each other's company. Don't bother talking about the negative things or the problems. Just take the time to really connect; even if the connection is short-lived, make it count. Encourage him to find solace in you, even on the days when he'd rather find a corner and get really quiet. Building a loving relationship takes work, but keeping that love and romance alive in times of adversity takes *hard* work. But your relationship is worth it.

## 3. DON'T JUDGE HIM

You have to remember that if money is tight, anything you say to him about money is going to amplify the situation in a negative way. A scenario: You come home from a tough day on the job to a mailbox full of bills, and before you can get into the house, the phone rings. It's the cable company, informing you once again that if you don't pay the bill, they're going to shut down service. Now, your man knows the bill is late but you hang up the phone and huff, "The cable bill is due."

In his mind, you might as well have said: "They're about to shut off the cable and if that happens, I won't be able to watch my shows after a hard day's work and I'll be doggone if I'm going to be the one going out here and getting the money and you're sitting here doing nothing while they take away the one thing I do to relax. You got us into this mess; what are *you* going to do to get us out of it?"

Unfortunately, it doesn't matter that this isn't what you intended; it's about the perceived attitude and tone, which can come across even when you don't realize you're doing it. He's already disappointed in himself, and he's just biding his time until you show that you're disappointed in him, too, until you let it be known that he's failing as a husband, father, and man because he's not providing for and protecting his family.

You know the bills are due and so does he; there's no need to bring it up unless you've got something concrete to offer in terms of how to dig yourselves out of the mess in which you've found yourselves. Otherwise, your words—whether they were said with attitude or meant as a simple observation—might just have him taking a trip down to the pawn shop, or dialing up a loan shark, or going down to the corner to do some things he has no business doing. All I'm saying is tread lightly.

## 4. FORM A TWO-PERSON CIRCLE

What's happening in your bank account—whether good or bad—is your business and your business only. Keep your financial information between the two of you, and share it with no one because believe me, no matter how much—or little—money you have, it's news to somebody. Tell a girlfriend that you went for the promotion on the job in hopes of earning more money because your man is out of work and "somebody's gotta do something," and the next thing you know, your entire world—family, friends, acquaintances, and enemies—will be standing at the ready to use that information against you. All you need to do is consider what happens when someone hits the lottery: as soon as the lottery winner pops up, and they're on the news with that oversized check, everybody's got their hands out. And in the instances when they lose all that money, spend it on foolish things, make some bad investments, get taken advantage of by people using and abusing them for their cash, the first thing everybody does is talk about how dumb they were. In other words, people get jealous and use whatever information they have to make you feel bad and themselves feel better. This hardly ever changes. Keep your information to yourself, and no one gets the opportunity to put your business in the street, pass judgment, or make you or your man feel bad about your financial situation.

Similarly: don't compare yourself with other couples. People specialize in making outward appearances shimmer; they're driving the bigger car or living in the fancier house, but chances are that something is probably wrong in their world too. Their car note may be two months behind, or they may be trying to work out a smaller payment on their mortgage loan. They're fronting and flexing and making you feel inferior for not having what they have, but they may well have problems even worse than yours. Whatever their financial business is, stay out of it and keep yours to yourself.

This is the advice I had for a listener who wrote into Steve Harvey.com asking for advice on how to handle family members and friends who started asking him for money after he and his wife opened a successful barbershop in their neighborhood. He'd made the mistake of telling a few people at a family get-together that leaving his regular job and starting his own business was the best financial decision he'd ever made—that he was making triple what he did working for someone else. Well, when people started passing that story around and eyeing the brisk business he was doing and seeing his wife driving around town in her new car, people started counting his money and making demands on his bank account. "I make good money, but I don't make enough to take care of everybody else. I'm just getting on my feet and people don't understand what it takes to run my business," he wrote. "How do I get them out of my pockets?"

I told him to start by keeping his financial business to

himself—to stop announcing his financial success at the family barbecues. No one but he and his wife need to know how much he makes, what they do with their money, where they put it, and how much they spend. "Take everyone out of it," I said. "And if anyone asks, keep the details to yourself, be as up front and clear as you possibly can: tell them your financial business is between you and your wife and that's that." And this is how it should be with all couples.

## IF YOUR MAN IS THE BREADWINNER . . .

Of course, there will be some relationships in which everything is fine financially and your man will be earning what he needs for the family while you set about the important work of keeping the house together. Please understand that even if you're not the primary breadwinner in your home—or a breadwinner at all—you still have power in your relationship. Most men I know give our ladies a lot of credit for holding down the fort. I know I need my wife to function and when I'm onstage performing, I frequently give her and the work she does at home a shout-out. A woman who is at home—I call her a home executive—is an incredibly valuable piece of the pie and has to be respected as such because she tends to things at home that make a man's life so much easier to handle. For instance, Marjorie is in charge at our house. People are constantly saying to me, "Hats off to you," because I married a woman with three kids and took them all in as my family, but what she did was no less. She's accepted my children from my previous marriages as if she gave birth to them herself. She's opened up our home to my kids and loved them, taken care of them, chastised them when they went astray. She's helped raise them, and while I'm going about my business, I know my kids are being well cared for and nourished emotionally and otherwise. That's major. More, I haven't a clue where the electric bill is, how much the cable costs, what it takes to keep my phone service running, how the groceries get purchased and cooked and set out on the table. Do you understand the peace this creates for a workingman? I can't put a price on what my wife does for me and our family. And it would be extremely unfair of me to act as if she somehow contributes to less of our financial stability because she isn't bringing home a check.

We're in the twenty-first century, and even women who aren't working have power in their relationship. A man can't put a price tag on what it means to return to a peaceful home, night after night, a place that's clean and full of food, a place with lights and electricity because the bills have been paid on time, a place where the kids are attending school and doing well. That's priceless. It allows us to flip into man mode and do what we have to do to make sure you and our family are well cared for.

If, however, your man is taking you for granted and isn't recognizing the value you bring to the relationship, I have some news for you: you can make him recognize it. This is what happened to a friend of mine when he made the mistake of taking his wife for granted. Every day, he would walk through the gate to a yard and house that was in order; nothing was out of place, the kitchen was always clean, the beds were always made, the kids were always fed, clothed, and clean. But he never said "Thank you for what you do" to his wife; he just acted as if this was par for the course.

One day, he came home and got deep into a conversation on the phone with one of his friends. His wife overheard him telling his friend, "Oh, she's great—living the life. She doesn't do anything; she's got her feet up on the sofa, watching soap operas. She doesn't do anything all day long. I tell you, she's got the life."

What did he say *that* for? The next day he came home and walked through the gate and the yard was all messed up; toys were strewn everywhere, bikes were lying in the grass, and sippy cups were out on the steps. He walked into a house where the sink was full of dishes and crayons were spread out across the carpet and tables. The kids were running around like banshees, and there was no dinner on the stove. The first thing out of his mouth was, "What have you been doing all day?"

"I didn't do a single thing today," she said simply, "just like you told your friend." And then she turned back to the television.

This went on for two weeks, with him coming home to a wreck of a house, no dinner, and kids running all over the place. Let's just say it didn't take him long to finally figure out what his wife really does throughout the day, and the value of it. She made it look so simple and easy, but really, her job was just as stressful, just as challenging, and just as valuable as his—albeit in a different way. And when they finally sat down to talk about it, she made clear her value: "What I do may not pay bills, but let me tell you what it does do: it gives you peace, good food, a clean house, well-behaved children, and a place to sit your coffee down and read your newspaper without interruption. If you don't want that, I can stop doing my job altogether. I don't mind watching these kids tear up this house."

This is all to say that sometimes you have to get a man's attention to make him recognize your worth. Maybe going about it the way my friend's wife did is a bit extreme, but there are ways to help him attach value to what you bring to the relationship. One of the easiest ways to make that happen is to write down your "to-do" list with checks next to all the things you've done during the course of the day, and then leave it somewhere where he can see it—on the kitchen table, in the bathroom next to his toothbrush, on his nightstand, next to the remote. This will be a nice subtle way of reminding him to respect your game.

If that doesn't get his attention, invite him to a sit-down and politely remind him of your value. Ask him if he saw your list, and if he thinks you're doing a good job. If he's not a fool, he will wake up and say, "Wow, yeah, what you do around the house is priceless." Tell him, "You know, I just want to thank you for what you do for this family; we make a fantastic team, right?" I assure you that he will turn around and thank you for a job well done too.

Sometimes you just have to get a man's attention—pull his coattails a little. We don't mean any harm, I promise you.

*I* know plenty of you are reading this with your finger in the back of your throat, trying to make yourselves gag over what

I'm telling women they need to do to make a man comfortable in a challenging financial relationship. But I feel the need to remind you: you have a certain set of skills that we do not possess, and you only serve yourself and your relationship with men better when you call on those skills and put them to use. Use your nurturing and communications skills—if you can use that skill set to get what you need and want out of others, there's no reason why you shouldn't put them to use with the person you love most, your mate. With good planning and a bit of luck, he'll eventually be back up on his feet and out of the fog—ego in check and grateful you hung in there and helped him through the storm. The two of you will be stronger and better for it.

# 12

‹━━◆━━›

## THE ART OF THE DEAL

### How to Get What You Want Out of a Man

My mother and father were married for sixty-four years.

There is a simple explanation for the longevity of their marriage.

My dad, Slick Harvey, recognized that he was not in charge and acted accordingly. This kept a smile on my mother's face, my father reasonably happy, and the marriage intact. Dad instinctively knew that in order to do what he wanted to do, he'd have to give my mother room to do what she wanted to do, say what she wanted to say, go where she wanted to go, and be who she wanted to be. He did this by practicing, subtly and masterfully, the art of negotiation—the art of the deal.

Take the time my mom announced she wanted to go pick up groceries at Southland Shopping Center, the new outlet of stores across town. She'd read about the opening in the paper and had just finished studying the grocery store circular when she decided she just had to have a carton of the Eagle brand eggs they were selling for thirty-nine cents per dozen at that particular chain. She didn't have to say it but one time, and my father was pulling on his shoes, coat, and hat and grabbing his keys. Her faithful chauffeur, he would drive her to church on Monday, Tuesday, Friday, and Sunday, as well as take her to the hairdresser when she needed to get her hair done and downtown when she saw a dress she wanted to buy or needed to get us kids some clothes for school. And now, my mother was adding the Southland Shopping Center to her list of shopping haunts.

What my brother and I didn't understand, at the tender ages of nineteen and eight, respectively, was why in the world my father wasn't asking what seemed the most obvious of questions: Why would anybody want to drive all the way across town to buy a dozen eggs at thirty-nine cents a dozen when the grocery store right up the street was selling the same carton of Eagle brand eggs for only twenty cents more? It just didn't make sense to us, though it was my brother who made the very foolish mistake of expressing his thoughts on the subject.

"I want to go to Southland because they have the eggs I want," my mother responded.

"But that's a good fifteen minutes out of the way, and you can get eggs for a reasonable price right down the street," he argued, with me behind him, nodding my head in agreement.

"I don't want those eggs down the street—I want the eggs over there at Southland," she insisted, pulling on her coat and walking toward the door. She was ready to go, and clearly was in no mood for arguing.

Now huffing in disbelief, he looked at my father and kept applying the pressure. "Wait, so let me get this straight: you're going to burn up all that gas running her across town? And spend two hours messing around in that store when you can get the same food down the street for a little bit more money? What kind of sense does that make?"

Finally, my father cut him off. "You through?" he asked, slowly.

My brother quickly shut his mouth and opened his ears.

"I could run her down to the store and let her get the fifty-nine-cent eggs, but that ain't what your mama wants. She wants to go over there to Southland, and so I'm going to take her to Southland. And if you don't shut the hell up, you're going to take her instead of me."

My father waited for my mother to get herself out the door and settled in the car before he continued. "You don't know nothing about women," he said, the bass in his voice taking over. "This isn't about logic, boy. It's what your mama wants. What will it hurt me to give her what she wants? I'm trying to go down there to the gas station and play pinochle, so if I want to do that, I'm going to run your mother around all day today, take her everywhere she wants to go so I can go where I want to go tonight."

The art of the deal.

On that very day, I learned one of the most important lessons my father could have ever taught me: happy wife, happy life. We men have been conditioned to conduct ourselves as if we run things, but the smart man knows it's really the woman of the house who sets the tone of the relationship and what goes on in the home. Sure, we know that most women don't have a problem bragging to their friends, "This is my man, he's the head of the household." Most of you will even take our last name and defer to us on some decisions. The idea is that if you do these things, on balance, you'll get most of what your heart desires. A woman will give a man an honorific as long as he puts her on a pedestal and gives her what *she* wants. No woman is going to sign up to call a man the head of the household if he's not acting like one—which encompasses making her feel honored, protected, and respected—and giving her, as I like to say, most of what she needs and a lot of what she wants. But guess what? The same is true for men—if anything, even more so.

We understand, respect, and live by the art of the deal. Everything for us is an exchange; I'll give you something if you give me something back. We've been cutting deals since we were little boys. "I like that black marble with the orange eye in it," a friend would say. "I'll trade you this green marble with the yellow spots, plus throw in a Hank Aaron baseball card if you give it to me, deal?" Go into any lunchroom in any school, USA, and you'll hear all kinds of deals being struck: "You got Pringles? Say man, I'll give you two dollars and a Reeses Peanut Butter Cup for those Pringles." The same thing is happening on the playground after school: "I bet you I can shoot twenty baskets faster than you. I'll even spot you five points. If I win, you have to give me two packs of Hubba Bubba when I see you tomorrow. Ready?"

Striking a deal is standard for us—it fits into our scheme of logic: you give something, you get something in return. That's the way it goes down for us at work, it's the way we deal with our siblings and cousins and other family members who consistently tap us for help, and it's certainly a part of our relationships with our friends. I'm not saying we're a selfish lot, by any stretch: I think the basic tenet of manhood—particularly for husbands, fathers, and men in committed relationships—is to give without expecting something in return; we provide for and protect our families in ways both big and small because we instinctively know that this is what an honorable man is *supposed* to do. And we know, too, that often those things will have to be done without expectation of getting anything in return. But I'll raise my hand high up in the air and cop to this one simple truth: a man is more likely to do things he doesn't want to do if he's going to get something out of it.

Just as you can use appreciation to motivate a man to do even more for you and your family (as explained in Chapter 10, "Show Your Appreciation"), you can accomplish the same by recognizing and implementing the principles of deal making in your relationship. It's very simple: if you want something from your man, offer up something in return. (And no, I'm not talking solely about sex, though you could get most men to wash the dishes, make all the beds, detangle your daughter's hair, and clean the refrigerator out weekly if they think they'll get the cookie in return.) Forget asking why you have to wheel and deal to get your husband to do things that women do without prompting. No matter how upset you get about it, no matter how many times you ask for an explanation, it's the way most of us are hardwired. This is the way men operate. Your job is to exploit this for your own advantage—to *figure out how to win within those confines*. Trust me on this one: understanding how to negotiate with your man will bring you untold joy. Just ask my wife, Marjorie—the master of the art of the deal in the Harvey household.

*M*arjorie and I are the parents of seven; she came to our relationship with three of her own and added them to my four. That's a houseful, no matter how you slice it, no matter how big your heart is, no matter how much time you have on your hands. Being a parent—a good parent—in that situation is daunting sometimes. When I get home, I don't want to deal with all the household drama, especially within ten minutes of setting foot in the front door. In my mind, I'm screaming, "I get that we need to speak about his grades, which are going in the wrong direction, and I understand that the little one wants to go to a friend's house for a sleepover and we don't trust the judgment of the girl's parents, and I know that the other one wants his friend to come over, which means I'm going to have to have a half-hour conversation with his father, whom I don't like. But I don't want to deal with this. I want to sit down, have a cigar, and zone out!" Yet as overwhelmed as I sometimes feel raising these kids, my wife has an even tougher go of it because she's the caretaker-in-chief of the Harvey household. For every hour I spend out on the road working, she's making the decisions and calling the shots for everything that goes down in our home. And so if I think caring for the kids is a daunting task, I can barely wrap my head around what it must be like for her, particularly when I'm not around.

Knowing this, however, doesn't necessarily move me to action when it comes to dealing with the particulars of child rearing. What gets me on the case is Marjorie's negotiating skills—her special ability to negotiate. She has nary a problem breaking it down: "Babe, if you spend a little time with the kids while I go shopping, I won't have a problem with you going golfing tomorrow."

Suddenly, I'm there to do whatever it is she needs, weighing in on every conversation, disciplining every kid.

It's an exchange. I do something I don't necessarily want to do, she gets the input and resources she needs, and I get a reward in return. She asks, I fulfill the request, we're both happy. Here's another example of how Marjorie works the art of the deal: I don't like musicals. I mean, *I can't stand them.* People are up on the stage yabbing about something I care nothing about and then all of a sudden they bust out into singing and dancing? Nope. This is not my idea of a good time.

Now, most of the time, Marjorie will gather up a few of her girlfriends and they'll go enjoy a musical together and then go out for dinner and do what they do when they're fellowshipping as friends. But on occasion, my wife will request that I attend a play or two with her, even though she knows I'd rather lie in a dentist's chair and have root canals performed simultaneously on all thirty-two of my teeth. And I will go because Marjorie practices the art of the deal: she will coax me into a suit and into the theater and later for a sushi dinner by promising me that she'll make it worth my while when we get back home. Let me tell you, I hear that offer and I can make it through anything. I can sit through forty songs in a five-hour play if my wife plants in my mind the image of her saying, "Taa daa!" when we get back to our bedroom later that night. I don't hear any music, and I can't tell you a single, solitary thing anyone up on that stage is saying; all I'm focused on is the treat Marjorie will have waiting for me back at the house.

And when she shows me—not only with the cookie but with genuine expressions of gratitude—that she's appreciative of my efforts to enjoy her passions, I know I have equity in the bank to enjoy my own hobbies and what little free time I have. If she gives me a moment to disappear into my office to catch a television show or flip through a magazine or just sit and be quiet, I make a point to free up time for Marjorie so that she can go get her nails done or get her hair fixed or go out for drinks with her girlfriends.

In other words, we've used a series of conversations and exchanges to strike deals that make our marriage run more smoothly. I promise you, talking it out and agreeing to make a series of exchanges to get what you want works like a charm but only if you're willing to have a civil conversation with your partner letting him know exactly what it is that you want. You can't expect him to intuit what you need, to come in the door and calculate before he's unknotted his tie that you've been in the house with the kids all afternoon, washed two loads of laundry, enrolled Junior in soccer and Missy in ballet, and that you could use, no, you absolutely need some me-time. Have a conversation with your man, tell him what you're willing to give him in exchange for what you need, strike the deal, and then enjoy the fruits of your labor. The same can be said of two people who come together for more personal, social partnerships. Say, for instance, you and one of your girlfriends decide to throw a little get-together for some of your other friends. Your girlfriend may be better at cooking and organizing the appetizers; you may be the expert at pairing wines with food and mixing up specialty drinks. To have a successful party, each of you has to talk about the kind of party you want to have and whom you're inviting, and then the two of you have to agree on what you'll contribute in order for your little get-together to be a success. Now, your girl may not necessarily want to cook all that food by herself, particularly if she's going to have to do it after a long, hard day's work. And you may not want to necessarily spend the entire party standing behind the bar, mixing drinks for a bunch of your drunken friends. But you'll both strike that deal—you'll provide the drinks if she hooks up the food—because you know that ultimately, your work will contribute to everyone having a fantastic time.

Every time you take your kids to the store, you strike a deal: "If you're quiet and behave while we're in the grocery store, I'll buy you a pack of gum when we get to the checkout." When you're at work, you strike deals: "If you gather up the statistics from last year's report, I'll plug in the numbers and do the calculations and together, we can present the new report to our manager." When you're on your college campus, with the goal of one day walking across that stage, you strike deals: "I'll help you research your paper and come up with a sound thesis if you help me figure out a better way to understand these math problems." When you're at the hairdresser or getting yourself a manicure or a massage, you're striking a deal: "Get my hair to look like Halle Berry's or Meg Ryan's and I'll give you a nice, fat tip and pass out a stack of your business cards to every woman I know!"

See, we strike deals all the time—in every little thing we do—with the hope that each partner will leave reasonably satisfied. Why not bring that into your relationship?

We know most of you don't want to have sex every night and that all the roles you play during the course of the day— employee, wife, homemaker, caretaker, friend, volunteer, chief boo-boo kisser—wear you out. You all know we don't want to change diapers and do dishes and read bedtime stories and do everything your way. But in the most successful of unions, partners are willing to change and shift and do things they don't necessarily want to do in order to work toward the greater good of the relationship.

For some of you the approach to a deal is a piece of cake. You are the very picture of diplomacy. But some of you have never been called subtle in your life. Start off the conversation in a way that doesn't put your man on the defensive. You don't want to start the conversation with him thinking he's about to be accused of falling down on the job. No guy is going to want to wheel and deal with you if he feels as if he's having a foot inserted into his behind. You know the saying "It's easier to catch bees with honey"? Well, nothing could be more true than when a woman is trying to negotiate with her man; no man wants to be blindsided by accusations about what he is and isn't doing. Besides, doing that will only make him fight or flee.

Instead, kick off your talk by flipping it on him: ask him what it is that you could be doing more of to help him. Let him know that you're happy he's your man and that you're his woman, but admit that you're not perfect and know you could be doing things that would make him happier. I know, I know—you *are* perfect. But your man doesn't think you are. He's just been afraid to tell you. If, however, you open the door to letting him express his true feelings without thinking he's going to be attacked for it, he's going to tick off a list of things he'd love to see more of from you—things that you can use in your negotiations. So stay calm, cool, and collected and be ready to accept whatever answer he gives you without having a knee-jerk reaction. He could be looking for more time to himself, more sex, more money in the savings account, more sex, more time to go golfing on the weekends or play basketball with the fellas, more sex. Whatever it is, listen carefully, and with an open mind.

And then blow his mind: tell him you agree that he should have more—more time to himself, more time with his boys, more time in the bedroom with you—and that you're willing to give him all those things if he agrees to do a few things for you. Now, you'll have his undivided attention because he's going to smell "payoff." That's when you can lay on him what you need. Maybe you'd be happier if you had a little more time to yourself, or maybe you need more help with the kids or the housework. Maybe you want him to be better about helping with the morning routine, or being more proactive when it comes to planning and taking you out for date nights. Whatever it is you need, come prepared to talk about it in a nonjudgmental way.

Once he's given his list and you've given yours, you've made the exchange. Now, both of you are clear about what you can offer in order to get some of what each of you need—the compromise you'll be willing to make. That's when you strike the deal.

Marjorie and I practice this even when we're on vacation. Just this past spring, we went to Cabo San Lucas in Mexico, just the two of us, so that we could get in some quality time together. But we made very clear to each other that we needed some much-needed me-time, too. Though she can't stand the smell of them, Marjorie knows how much I enjoy a good cigar; it relaxes me like nothing else can. I pull the cigar smoke into my mouth and hold it right there while I breathe in and out, careful not to let the smoke go down into my lungs. And then I blow it out and take another puff. If it's a fine cigar—one that's not bitter, that has a smooth taste—I'm satisfied, happy. Knowing this, Marjorie kept my cigars ordered and made sure that I had plenty on hand so that I could be fully relaxed. In exchange, I made sure she had strawberries and her favorite drink replenished every time she got low, because that fruit and drink relaxed her. We both made a deal, too, to give each other space; she gave me the okay to go golfing, and in exchange, I let her spend a day by herself at the spa. When we came back together our time was enhanced, electric. In other words, we had the conversation, we made the exchange, we struck the deals, and we saw big-time results in our relationship.

You don't have to go to Cabo, order up expensive cigars, or keep fancy drinks flowing to get what you need from your man. All you have to do is practice the art of the deal, negotiate diplomatically. Take some cues from these specific discussions to help kick off some important deals of your own.

## EXAMPLE #1

**THE CONVERSATION**: You know honey, I get that you're not a fan of reading bedtime stories to the kids and tucking them in. After a long day of doing so much for everyone else—dealing with the boss, taking that long ride home, running to the grocery store to pick up the milk—it's hard to come home and do anything but fall into the most comfortable chair you can find and zone out. I totally get that. At the same time, I wish there were a way for me to take a quiet bath in the evening, even if it's just for a couple nights during the week, just so that I could unwind from my long days at work, the commute, dinner prep, and homework assistance.

**THE EXCHANGE**: If you take over the bedtime routine with the kids for two nights a week—get them into their pajamas, read them a story, and tuck them into bed—I can run some bathwater and light some candles and have myself a glass of wine and relax. I can do the same for you on the other nights when you come in from work, so that you can enjoy some quiet time by yourself before you turn in for the evening.

**THE DEAL**: The more time I get to unwind and relax and get in some quiet time without having to get the kids down, the higher the chances that I'll be in the mood to spend some quality time with you.

**THE RESULT:** You'll get a break from the kids; your husband will get more cookie.

## EXAMPLE #2

**THE CONVERSATION:** Babe, we spend an awful lot of time with each other yet when we have time with our friends, we come back renewed from that time and look forward to each other's company. Wouldn't it be nice if we got to bond with the other people in our lives that we love? You know the saying: Absence makes the heart grown fonder.

**THE EXCHANGE:** If you let me go out with my girls on one Friday night out of the month, I'll let you hang with your boys one Saturday night out of the month, and on Sundays, we can spend quality time together—just me and you.

**THE DEAL:** The more time each of us gets to spend bonding with our friends and finding some joy away from each other, the more we'll be able to connect when we come back together again.

**THE RESULT:** The two of you will ultimately enjoy spending time together.

## EXAMPLE #3

**THE CONVERSATION:** You know, we spend so much of our money on bills and the mortgage and the car notes and all the other things we have to pay to keep our lives running, we don't have anything left over for ourselves. Wouldn't it be nice to enjoy the fruits of our labor every once in a while?

**THE EXCHANGE:** If I focus on paying off one of our credit cards, and you take your lunch to work more often and take the train to the city instead of driving our gas guzzler to work, we could save a good three hundred dollars a month in food expenses and credit card bill interest.

**THE DEAL:** We can divvy up the savings—a quarter of it you can spend the way you see fit; a quarter of it I can spend on anything I want, and we can save the rest to get something special for the two of us.

**THE RESULT:** Both of you get a little extra spending money in your separate accounts, and get to work together toward a mutual goal.

See? Everybody wins. Keep this one thing in mind, though: you can't strike the deal and renege. We men are sticklers for the "but you said you would" demands, so you cannot walk away having gotten what you wanted without giving him what he wants. Of course, the same is true for us men. In order for the deal to work, both parties have to hold up their end of the bargain; there must be accountability. This is where your standards and requirements—the ones I wrote about in *Act Like a Lady, Think Like a Man*—come into play. Just like you did when you were dating and letting your man know up front what you wanted, needed, and expected out of your relationship, all the things that you required of a man in order for him to win your time, attention, and affection, you will have to require your man to live up to the agreement he's made. You can't let him put the kids to bed a couple days every week for three weeks, and sit passively back as he cuts back to once a week for the next two weeks, and then stops helping with the kids' routine altogether, while you're still pulling out the Saturday night bells and whistles and the monkey show on a Tuesday. No monkeys need to be coming out unless he keeps up the end of the deal he struck. Otherwise, you'll both be right back to the frustration you were feeling before you learned to negotiate.

You deserve better.

## USING THE ART OF THE DEAL TO MAINTAIN STANDARDS AND REQUIREMENTS IN A RELATIONSHIP

In the beginning of your relationship, you weren't passing out the cookie to a man who wasn't treating you right; you gave it to him based on his meeting your standards and requirements and doing nice things for you. But as you get deeper into the relationship, your man will slowly pull back on the tactics, treats, and attention he used to win you over. It's just what we do; capturing you was hard work and once we have you, we get comfortable putting in less work on the romantic side of things because we're busy providing for and protecting you and we soon find out that even if we don't break a sweat meeting your standards and requirements in the bedroom, you don't usually complain. You give based on your emotions, not your mate's actions. And so he chills. He's not rubbing your feet anymore and he hasn't licked your back since 1979, but he's still over there requiring you give him your all—and that leads to frustration, chiefly, yours.

How do you get him back on board? Talk. Men are not mind readers, and we will continue on as is if you don't tap us on the shoulder and make clear what you want—just like you did when we first approached you. You simply cannot afford to let your guard down if you want to be happy. Open the conversation with a compliment; tell him in a sexy, sly way that you appreciate what he's doing—holding down the family, bringing home the bacon, being a strong man for you and yours. But then toss in the honesty: tell him you really miss the things he used to do to you that drove you up and down the wall. Reminisce a little—remind him of that time you swung from the chandeliers, and the time you arrived home to rose petals on the bed, and the hot times you used to have in the hotel during your quick, romantic getaways. I promise you, he will be all ears during this conversation. Getting good cookie, after all, is our favorite subject. We hear, "Hmm—she's talking about me driving her up the wall—it must be about to happen this evening. Yes!" And he'll start thinking about what he can do to make you feel that way again.

Seal the deal by telling him what you would love to show him in exchange for getting some of that spark back. Now, he's saying to himself, "If I do this, I'll get that. Where do I sign?" It's the reward system—works every time, even in the romance side of your life. You can't walk into this thing saying, "You don't hold me anymore, you don't look at me like you did before!" because what you'll get back is, "Oh yeah? Well, you're only half cooking, you haven't worn a thong in twenty years, and all your underwear has lint balls on it. Who wants a part of that?"

This is my way of saying, use your feminine wiles in a way that benefits you, even after you've got him.

# PART IV

## Questions and Commandments

# ASK STEVE

## More Quick Answers to the Burning Questions You've Always Wanted to Ask

When *Act Like a Lady, Think Like a Man* was published, I traveled all across the country talking to women about the ways of men, and at each event, I invited my audience to submit the burning questions they have about the opposite sex. Here, I give quick and candid answers to the queries that repeatedly found their way into the mix.

### 1. DO MEN BELIEVE IN LOVE AT FIRST SIGHT?

SH: Yes, we do believe in love at first sight, but it's based purely on the sight. We're just in love with what we see initially. But that love can easily go away—you can start out winning and slowly lose this guy once he gets to know you. He may decide in his mind you don't sound like you look, you don't think like you look, you don't act like you look, and you don't have what you look like you have. That's what kills the romance. False advertisement. And sometimes, we just change our minds about it, and it's no fault of your own.

## 2. WHAT ARE THE TOP TEN PLACES TO MEET MEN?

**SH:** I can't tell you that because there is no one set place. You can meet a man anywhere. I knew a man who married the woman he rear-ended in a car accident. I know another man who married his divorce lawyer. Another one of my friends remarried his first wife, and another one married the woman his son was dating. You can meet and fall in love with anyone anywhere, and it's ridiculous to limit yourself to a few places. This is why I say in the "Presentation Is Everything" chapter that you have to be prepared; if you're going to the ice cream store, the Laundromat, the hospital, the park, the gym, there might be a man there just for you. Be open to anything, anywhere.

## 3. IS IT A TURNOFF FOR MEN TO DATE DIVORCED WOMEN?

**SH:** No. Nothing is a turnoff if we're attracted to you. No matter what, if he likes you, he's going to approach you and see where the encounter leads.

## 4. WHAT DO MEN NEED AFTER MARRIAGE TO STAY SEXUALLY INTERESTED?

**SH:** We need variety and spontaneity. There isn't a guy living who doesn't like that. If you don't know this about your man, it's because he hasn't told you yet. But keep doing the same thing and you'll see how that affects your love life. Wouldn't you be bored if, after years of being together, your man was still bringing the same flowers and playing the same songs and saying the same things he brought, played, and said when he first met you? Wouldn't you just love it if, out of the blue, he did something different and special for you? Well, men are no different. If you want to get him sexually interested, toss a sombrero, some high heels, and roses on the nightstand and scribble the words, "Anywhere, Anytime" on a piece of paper. That'll get him interested, I promise you that. Meet him in the garage and get something going before he even gets out of his car. Get in some loving in a store's dressing room. Just be different. He'll respond every time.

## 5. WHEN A MAN SAYS "IT'S NOT YOU, IT'S ME" OR "I'M NOT READY FOR YOU" AS AN EXCUSE FOR BREAKING OFF A RELATIONSHIP, IS HE JUST SPORT FISHING?

**SH:** Not necessarily. Sometimes a guy is being honest. Sometimes he's not willing or simply cannot give you what you want, and honorable guys will tell women that. If he says, "I'm not for you, you deserve better," take his words as a blessing. Some women stay there, trying to force the issue, or continue to invest in a man who's clearly told her he's not ready for a serious relationship. Obviously, you can't be committed to making the relationship work by yourself. So be smart about it: thank him, tell him you appreciate his honesty, and go on about your business.

## 6. FOR SINGLE MOTHERS RAISING BOYS, WHAT IS THE NUMBER ONE THING WE CAN TEACH THEM TO HELP THEM FORM HEALTHY RELATIONSHIPS WITH THE OPPOSITE SEX?

**SH:** Avoid sharing with your young sons the reasons you and your man aren't together. Doing this accomplishes little more than dumping information onto a person who is too young to process it. Instead, talk to him constantly about how you like to be treated—what makes you feel good as a woman and a mother. He'll remember that you like to have doors opened for you, chairs pulled out, a person who listens respectfully when you're talking, and who tells the truth when he's asked questions—all things big and small that he'll need to remember and practice when he gets into his own relationships with women. The best thing you can do for your sons, though, is get them strong male role models they can emulate—men who can supplement the incredible job single moms everywhere are doing with their boys.

## 7. WHY DO MEN CONTINUE TO LIE, EVEN AFTER THEY'VE BEEN CAUGHT AND CONFRONTED, AND ESPECIALLY WHEN THE TRUTH WILL DO?

**SH:** Because we know the truth will absolutely not do anything for us except get us deeper into trouble and hurt your feelings more. What you need to understand is that sometimes that lie, that withholding of all the information, is his way of protecting you from getting more mad, scornful, and resentful than you already are when you *suspect* we've done something wrong. Our lie, in effect, is really about damage control; we're not giving the whole truth because doing so would add more fuel to the fire. You're already fired up with the information you have. It doesn't make sense to give you more information. No man is going to do that. Feel how you want to feel about it, but really, he's trying to have some decency about his mess. You may know about three indiscretions, but do you think he's really going to disclose to you that there were thirty more? No way. Because your response will only intensify. We're sparing your feelings and keeping ourselves out of deeper trouble.

## 8. WHY DO MEN STOP CALLING WITHOUT ANY EXPLANATION FOR WHY THEY'RE NOT COMMUNICATING ANYMORE?

**SH:** Because we're done. You need closure, but men don't; we just need it to be over. We don't need to know why it didn't work, we don't want to consider trying it again; we don't question the rationale behind our decision. We didn't like talking while we were together; we're not about to become the Great

Communicator now that we've broken up. So women would do themselves well to let it go. It's over—move on.

## 9. WHY ARE MEN SO UNCOMFORTABLE SHOWING THEIR FEELINGS?

**SH:** Because from boyhood through our journey to manhood, we were never taught to express our feelings. Our parents, our extended families, our teachers, our friends—everyone tells boys not to emote like girls, to be men, to stop all that crying. We are raised to hold in and hide our emotions. And so we learn to be silent and keep our emotions in check. Once we get into a relationship with a woman we're deficient in the art of communicating with women because we've never been expressive in our lives. Women learn and express themselves differently; you get to walk together with your girls arm in arm, you dance together at the club, you hug each other, touch each other's faces while you're talking. We're not touching any man's face or kissing him on the cheek. We are taught the exact opposite all our lives and we grow comfortable with it. And honestly, I don't think you need to break that pattern with your man. You can't sit around the house crying with your man. You know as well as I do that the moment he started bawling, you'd be on the phone with your girls, saying, "This man is crying harder than I am!" You want your man to be a man and we can't be touchy-feely with our emotions when we're charged with manning up for the family. It's a skill set you need your man to have.

## 10. HOW DO I GET MY MAN TO BE MORE SPONTANEOUS?

**SH:** By giving him a reason to be spontaneous. It's very simple: if there is a reward in it, we'll do it. This is nothing new. When we're good students, we want the gold star; when we're in a race, we want a gold medal; when we get a promotion, we want a raise. Why in the world would we give up the reward system in a relationship? As I wrote in the Chapter 12, "The Art of the Deal," if you make a promise in exchange for that spontaneity, we'll give you spontaneity all damn day. And know that there is only one payoff: we don't want a pack of socks or underwear or a hand-drawn bath full of rose petals or a cash advance. All we want is some cookie. Give that to us and you're golden.

## 11. DO MEN PREFER SEX WITH NEW PARTNERS OVER SEX WITH WOMEN WITH WHOM THEY'VE HAD A LONG-TERM RELATIONSHIP?

**SH:** We can get new sex from the woman with whom we're in a long-term relationship. Variety is the spice of life. Take that short answer and pack it wherever you want to pack it.

## 12. WHY DON'T MEN LIKE PUBLIC DISPLAYS OF AFFECTION— HOLDING HANDS, KISSING, AND SO ON?

**SH:** That's not true at all. I hold my wife's hand everywhere I go and kiss her in restaurants all the time. If your man doesn't want to do that, maybe he doesn't like holding *your* hand or kissing you. Maybe he doesn't want anyone—his wife, his girlfriend, prospective love interests—to know you're together. If you want him to be more affectionate in public, take his hand, kiss him when the mood suits you (and it's appropriate), and hug him when you need one. If he cares about you, he'll return the affection, no matter who is watching.

## 13. IF A MAN BRINGS ME AROUND HIS FRIENDS, DOES THAT MEAN HE'S REALLY INTO ME?

SH: It could be, but it's a sure sign that he's not into you if you don't ever get around his friends. If he's not proud of you or wants to keep what he has with you under wraps, he won't ever bring you around his boys.

## 14. WHAT MAKES MEN HAPPY?

SH: Cookie.

## 15. WHAT IS A MAN'S IDEA OF A GOOD WOMAN?

SH: Well, it varies from man to man. Some men want a woman who is working and contributing financially to the relationship. Some men want women to stay home and raise the family. Some men want someone who is stunning and supersmart. But at the end of the day, we all want and need the same thing out of our woman, no matter how much she's willing to contribute to the bank account, do around the house, or dress up to make herself look superattractive: men have to have a woman who is loyal, supportive, and willing to give us cookie on a regular basis. If you're missing any one of those things, then you're not going to be a good woman for any man.

## 16. WHAT ARE THE TOP THINGS MEN LOOK FOR TO DETERMINE IF YOU'RE MARRIAGE MATERIAL?

**SH:** First, let me put this out there: you're never going to be marriage material to everybody. Please take that pressure off yourself. You're only going to be marriage material to the man who is looking for you. If you are fulfilling his requirements, you become marriage material. But if that guy isn't looking to you for a long-term relationship, it doesn't matter how much cooking and cleaning you do, how good the sex is, or how much intelligence, money, and know-how you bring to the table, he's not going to propose. I can tell you that the women who are marriage material all have one thing in common, though: they all require that they be married. I don't know a single woman who just surprisingly got married—like, "Oh, how did this happen?" The way and day he proposes may be a surprise, but you knew the day would come because you made it a requirement.

## 17. WHY DO MEN BECOME SUCH A BORE AFTER MARRIAGE?

**SH:** Often it's because you have started accepting the same old thing, and so he has no reason to do anything exciting anymore. Put that reward system in place and you'll get all manner of excitement pumped back into your relationship. Want to go out to dinner more? Say so. Want to go to more concerts or long walks in the park? Tell him. Then reward him when he does these things for you.

## 18. ARE MEN TURNED OFF BY A WOMAN WHO SPENDS A LOT OF TIME PURSUING HER CAREER AND FOCUSING ON HER KIDS?

SH: No, they are not. And you should never stop pushing yourself or taking proper care of your kids to please any man. If you're going to work to take care of your bills and you are involved in your kids' education and extracurricular activities, if you're working hard to build a good life for them, why, it would be irrational to stop doing these things for a man's benefit. That's just foolish. A real man who meets an attractive woman who isn't doing these things will want nothing to do with her. And you should reject any man who has a problem with you doing what you're supposed to do to take care of yourself and your family.

## 19. HOW DO MEN FEEL ABOUT ONLINE DATING?

SH: It depends on the man, just like it does the woman. But it's really starting to be nearly unavoidable because technology is such a valuable and pervasive tool in people's lives. I believe you can save yourselves a lot of time and pain if you get online and talk to a guy before you meet him in person; you can learn a lot before you waste your time with time-consuming dates. And don't underestimate the power of Google and sites like Free ID Search. All of these, in conjunction with online dating, are smart ways to connect with the opposite sex and really get to know whom you're dealing with before you meet them in person.

## 20. WHAT ARE SOME GOOD TIPS FOR FINDING LOVE ONLINE? DO THE SAME RULES APPLY?

**SH:** The rules are the same. You have to take your time, you have to get to know a person, you have to ask the right questions, you have to dig until you know the truth, and you have to be careful. And, most important, you have to remember that it's not what they say, it's what they do, even if it's online.

## 21. DO MEN THINK IT'S ACCEPTABLE TO DATE THEIR FRIEND'S EX?

**SH:** Most men consider this taboo. Does it happen? Sure. But most men know this is a line you don't want to cross with a true friend because, in our eyes, you will always be his girl and we don't ever start something with our friend's woman. You're virtually guaranteed to get your feelings hurt when you do that.

## 22. HOW DO MEN FEEL ABOUT LONG-DISTANCE RELATIONSHIPS? DO THEY WORK FOR MEN?

**SH:** They can work if the man wants to make it work. The number one challenge is trust: Is he who he really says he is and is he doing what he says he's doing? There's not a whole lot of ways to check up on that. What the two of you have to do is determine if you can work on coming together and, in the meantime, set standards and rules that will work for both of you. But be clear: there aren't a lot of ways to check up on him when he's not living near you. Don't be naive about it: Is he sitting around twiddling his thumbs, waiting for the next time he sees you? Or is someone providing him a bit of satisfaction while he waits for you?

## 23. HOW DO MEN GET OVER GETTING HURT IN RELATIONSHIPS?

**SH:** For the most part, we move on. We go get somebody else. Are we scarred? Sure, but we'll go forward, scarred, beat up, teeth cracked, bones broken. We have a moment of pause, a moment of regret, and then we get over it the best way we know how: by finding someone else. We understand very clearly that the best way to get over the last relationship is to start something cracking with someone new. We understand that life goes on.

## 24. DOES AGE REALLY MATTER TO MEN?

**SH:** If it's a guy who's younger debating about whether he should see an older woman, age matters. We're trying to determine what she's going to look like in ten years, what we'll be able to enjoy together, and if she's going to age well. In reverse, age really matters, as well. Once you're a grown adult male, you're conscious about how young a woman is. If a man has his act together and is mature, he's not looking for someone to raise. He wants someone who is already grown. Really, though, the difference in age range that a man finds acceptable is really up to him.

## 25. HOW DO MEN FEEL ABOUT WOMEN GOING THROUGH THEIR PHONES AND USING OTHER INVESTIGATIVE TACTICS TO FIGURE OUT IF THEIR MAN IS BEING TRUE?

**SH:** Your man will hate you.

## 26. IF A MAN TELLS YOU HE NEEDS A "BREAK," DOES THAT MEAN YOU'RE BROKEN UP FOR GOOD?

**SH:** That's the biggest warning sign a man can give. When you hear that, wave the white flag, grab the kids, and get to your mama's house because what he's just done is broken it to you softly. He's telling you he's going to stop calling you, he doesn't want to see you, and he's taking a break from sex—with you. He's tired of you. That's the warning shot that the end is here—that he's going on with his life. And you should too.

## 27. HOW DO GUYS FEEL ABOUT "HINTS" FROM WOMEN WHO ARE ATTRACTED TO THEM?

**SH:** We're cool with the hints and with direct flirting, too. The only time we don't like it is when we're not interested.

## 28. DO MEN TREAT FRIENDS WHO BECOME LOVE INTERESTS THE SAME WAY AS THEY DO STRANGERS WHO BECOME LOVE INTERESTS?

**SH:** Look, the only reason you were friends in the first place was because he didn't think there was any chance of your relationship developing romantically. Know that he's been eyeballing you from day one; no man is looking to be just a friend. He wanted you from the start. He settled for friendship because he didn't think you would have him otherwise. The moment you let him be more than that, a line has been crossed and all bets are off if it doesn't work out between the two of you—unless, of course, you both agree that it's better for the two of you to go back to being friends. But it won't be easy to go back to that space once you cross the line and become lovers.

## 29. ARE MEN INFLUENCED BY FRIENDS WHEN IT COMES TO COMMITMENT?

**SH:** Yes, absolutely. If you're a guy in a serious relationship and all your friends are single, wilding out, and sport fishing (see the glossary), when you hang out with them, association brings on participation. After a while, it's hard to behave. But this works in reverse, too: if all your friends are in committed relationships and you're the one wilding out, you at least try not to do wrong when you're with them. That's the case with my circle of friends: my four buddies I travel with are committed in their relationships and the single men who play around know that when they come around us, they have to shut down or hide the craziness.

## 30. DO MEN LIKE ROMANCE? WHAT DO THEY FIND ROMANTIC?

**SH:** Yes, men like romance and men will continue to be romantic once it's required of them. Just know, though, that romance for us usually means it's going to lead to something. I'm sorry—that's the way we think. We have to be reminded, sometimes, that cuddling is just that, cuddling. When a woman is romancing a man, we're always going to think, "Okay, here's another shot at getting some cookie." Sometimes we get it, sometimes we don't, but we're working on a different mechanism, here.

We're thinking: "She's being romantic for a reason." Is that right or fair? No. But that's the way we think. So be romantic at your own peril.

## 31. CAN MEN CONTINUE TO BE FRIENDS WITH AN EX WITHOUT BEING SEXUALLY ATTRACTED TO HER?

**SH:** Yes, we can be just friends with her. Most divorces end up kind of rough, and there's often genuine hatred between the two. But we can move past the hate and be cordial with the ex and not be sexually attracted to her, for sure. If the ex is someone we dated, however, it can be a little more tricky, especially if a man is in a committed relationship. Under those circumstances, I don't recommend being friends with the ex. No one erases all the memories, so hanging around someone with whom you've been intimate can be akin to playing with fire. You know what men are after, and you know if a man has had it once before, it's hard for him to walk away from it if it's being offered again. I'm not suggesting that men don't have the willpower to be faithful, but I do think it's just better for everyone involved to keep the distance.

## 32. DO MEN GET AS BOTHERED AS WOMEN DO WHEN WE FORGET BIRTHDAYS, ANNIVERSARIES, AND SO ON?

**SH:** We won't let our displeasure be seen, but when important moments are forgotten, we do get hurt. We want to be celebrated just as you do.

## 33. IF A MAN TEXTS YOU CONSISTENTLY, DOES THAT MEAN HE'S INTO YOU?

**SH:** It means nothing. That same text can be sent to a bunch of women at the same time and he can forward it to a half dozen more. A man shows he's "into" you by communicating with you in traditional ways—via a phone call, an in-person talk, a date. Text messages don't cut it. Men who are interested in you want to be in your space, see your face.

## 34. WHY ARE MEN SO PICKY?

**SH:** Aren't you picky when it comes to men? See, here's what we're not about to do: we're not changing our standards. The moment you're not keeping it up, the moment you're not pulling your weight, the moment you don't fit into what we're looking for, we're pulling up stakes. We want what we want and we're not going to "settle" for a wife. You all would do well to take a page from men and stop compromising your standards and get exactly what you want in the man you deserve as well.

# FOR THE MEN . . . TEN COMMANDMENTS TO PLEASING A WOMAN

## 1. Thou Shalt Give Her Free Time.

Make the time for her to be able to take a class or pursue a hobby that she's been putting off because she's too busy with work and the kids to spend quality time doing something she loves.

## 2. Thou Shalt Remember the Small Things.

Rub her back and feet, run her bathwater and give her quality "alone time," without obligation to give you some cookie for your troubles.

### 3. Thou Shalt Consistently Find New Ways to Say I Love You.

Love notes go a long way. Slip one in her wallet, briefcase, or lunch bag just because; she'll appreciate that you were thinking about her and told her you love her without prompting.

### 4. Thou Shalt Chip In.

Wash the dishes, do a load of laundry, clean the bathroom, or do some other chore she usually handles. If you can't or don't want to handle it yourself, hire someone to do it for you. That'll be one less thing she'll have to do, and she'll be grateful for the help.

### 5. Thou Shalt Help with the Kids.

Offer to put them to bed a couple nights a week or run them to their extracurricular activities. She could probably use the help.

### 6. Thou Shalt Embrace the Art of Foreplay.

If candlelight and soft music used to get her in a romantic mood but you haven't used either of them in years, get back to romancing her. She'll appreciate the effort and respond in kind.

## 7. Thou Shalt Respect Her Schedule.

Sure, you should be able to get in a little overtime at work or go for a three-day golf weekend with the guys without being hassled about it, but it's better for everyone involved if you co-ordinate your schedule with hers instead of assuming that she will just handle the house, the kids, and whatever else is coming the family's way while you're out having a good time.

## 8. Thou Shalt Send Her Roses, Just Because.

Don't wait for birthdays, anniversaries, and holidays to shower her with the things she loves. A simple bouquet of flowers or a pack of her favorite candy is a kind gesture that will show her you were thinking about her.

## 9. Thou Shalt Remember the Golden Rule.

You can be happy or you can be right.

## 10. Thou Shalt Always Take Her Side.

Of course, your mother taught you that she's always right. The woman you sleep with at night must feel like you've got her back, no matter who she's going up against. She'll give you that same support, too.

# GLOSSARY OF STEVE'S TERMS

>——⊱◈⊰——<

**WHAT DRIVES MEN:** Who they are (title), what they do (job, career), and what they make.

**THE THREE Ps:** The three distinct ways men show their love to their mates—by providing, professing (telling a woman and everyone she knows that she is his girlfriend/lady/wife), and protecting.

**THE COOKIE:** Sex.

**THE THREE THINGS EVERY MAN NEEDS:** Support, loyalty, and the cookie.

**THE NINETY-DAY RULE:** A probationary period in which a woman forgos having sex with a man until she figures out whether he's really into her and what his intentions are for the relationship.

**WE HAVE TO TALK:** The four scariest words a man will ever hear.

**FIX-IT MODE:** When men forgo talking, pondering, and mulling over a problem and instead figure out what the problem is and do what it takes to make the problem go away with as little drama as possible.

**THROWBACK:** A party girl who has no rules, requirements, or respect for herself and doesn't make any demands on prospective suitors, or a woman who is clueless about how to deal with men.

**SPORT FISHING:** When a man dates a woman knowing that he has no intention of making any long-term commitments with her.

**KEEPERS:** Women who have standards and requirements for their relationships, carry themselves with respect, and demand potential suitors treat them with respect.

**STANDARDS AND REQUIREMENTS:** The expectations women have and the rules they set for potential mates interested in dating them.

**THE FIVE QUESTIONS:** Queries every woman should ask a man to determine what he wants out of his life and his relationship with her. They ultimately help women determine right away what values a man has and how she fits into his plans. The questions include: What are your short-term goals? What are your long-term goals? What are your views on relationships? What do you think about me? and How do you feel about me?

# ACKNOWLEDGMENTS

I would like to pay a debt of gratitude to some amazingly helpful people. My editor and publisher, Dawn Davis, somehow believed I could write a book in the first place . . . and then backed up that belief with a work ethic I've seen only a few times in my life. Jill Jamison, a new hire with invaluable insight, sat in every single writing session to help form my focus group. A special thanks to Shirley Strawberry, who, with her inquisitive nature and relentless questioning, pushed me to dig deeper and deeper, to be more thorough for my female readers; she was also there for all the read-throughs, even reading all the drafts out loud to me and refusing to let me nod off in the final rereads.

This book also does not exist without the millions of readers who bought my first book, *Act Like a Lady, Think Like a Man*. Your follow-up and seminar questions motivated me to go further into the minds of my male friends, giving birth to what I think is a book that is as important as the first book. The two together offer quite a bit of knowledge.

## ACKNOWLEDGMENTS

My business partner and best friend, Rushion McDonald, works behind the scenes, but his work ethic, savvy, and promotional skills have aided in not only my publishing endeavors, but also in the many hard-fought battles he and I have engaged in over the past twenty years. Nothing we've done has been easy, but it's all been so rewarding. Thank you, my friend.

And to Denene Millner, who has typed, edited, and laughed through this entire project, helping me to put my unique thought processes and even more unique speech patterns into readable prose: Thank you for your guidance, questions, and devotion to this project. Thank you, thank you, thank you.

To my family, who are too many to mention, Thank you. I love all of my kids.

And now for my favorite part: My wife, Marjorie. . . . I can't put on this page what she means to me. I've evolved into the person I am over the last five years because of this wonderful gift that was given to me named Marjorie. She proves God really does know what we need more than we do. In all my life and in all my imagination I never knew this could exist for me. She allows me to be better; she encourages me to be better; and here's the kicker: she expects me to be better. And on top of all that she appreciates it when I am. And that causes me to walk through walls and any hellfire for her. I have a few hundred things I could say about her but I will save that for another book. It's because of Marjorie that I'm able to share with you so much of my own journey. She is "the bomb." I love my girl, Marjorie.

WITHOUT GOD, I WOULD BE LOST. YOUR DIRECTIONS HAVE BEEN FLAWLESS. YOU HAVE

TAKEN ME PLACES FAR BEYOND MY DREAMS. YOU HAVE GIVEN ME MORE THAN HOPE. YOU HAVE SURPASSED ALL MY EXPECTATIONS AND AT THE SAME TIME OPENED MY MIND TO RECEIVE EVEN MORE INSPIRATION. I DONT KNOW WHERE ALL THIS IS GOING BUT I AM WILLING TO FOLLOW BE-CAUSE YOUR VISION AND GUIDANCE IS OFF THE CHAIN. SO PLEASE, PLEASE DONT STOP DOING WHAT YOU DO.

—Your imperfect soldier, Steve. . . . GOD is not through with me yet.